INVITATION TO HEALING

Invitation
to
Healing

ROY LAWRENCE

KINGSWAY PUBLICATIONS
EASTBOURNE

ISBN 0 86065 025 1

Printed in Great Britain for
KINGSWAY PUBLICATIONS LTD
*Lottbridge Drove, Eastbourne, E. Sussex BN23 6NT by
Hunt Barnard Printing Ltd., Aylesbury, Bucks.*

CONTENTS

Migraine at its worst is an agonizing thing, and Jack suffered from it regularly.

I can picture him on the last occasion on which I saw him with a migraine attack. He was lying in a darkened room, because the light hurt him. His eyes had almost vanished out of sight behind the puffy slits of his eyelids. He exuded pain from every pore.

A message had come to the Vicarage asking me to visit him and administer a 'laying on of hands'. I should explain that there is nothing remarkable or extraordinary about my hands, no psychic gift, no science-fiction-like force projected from them. But I believe that the church is the body of Christ and that it is commissioned to administer the touch of Christ at all levels in society, and not least to those who are sick.

So I went to Jack's house and was shown into his bedroom. He was clearly in no condition for social pleasantries and so, without any waste of time, we set about the work of Christian healing. Putting one hand around the back of Jack's head and the other on his poor sweating forehead, I prayed in the name of Jesus that my hands might be Jesus's hands, and that his touch would stimulate the healing power of the Holy Spirit.

Nothing spectacular happened on the spot. Gradually Jack's migraine passed. Some months later I left the neighbourhood because my Bishop had asked me to leave the parish of St. George's, Hyde, and to go to the Merseyside parish of St. Stephen's, Prenton, on the edge of Birkenhead.

It was about two years after my visit to Jack that he came to Birkenhead to visit me. He wanted to tell me that during that period for the first time in years he had been completely

free from any sort of severe migraine. He found that whenever he felt that a migraine might be coming on, if he went
to church and sat there, quietly aware of the presence of
God, then the threat passed.

That is just one of the stories which did not find a place in
Christian Healing Rediscovered, the book which I was asked
to write before leaving Hyde.

A book is in many ways a frustrating thing. For one thing,
after it has been finished, all sorts of things come to mind
which might have been included, all sorts of stories which
might have been told. Also, a book is a static thing, whereas
life is not. I can now see that many of the stories told in that
book were incomplete and that there is much more to tell
than I knew at the time.

Life moves on, and I have moved on myself. Christian
experience is never static. If I am in any way open to the
Holy Spirit, I must constantly be in a learning situation,
open to new development, new awareness. My family and I
are now settled in our new home in a new district. This has
brought new experiences, new opportunities, new discoveries.

So now, after my first book, let us journey a little further
in that exploration of the mystery of healing to which I
believe God calls every church and every Christian.

ACKNOWLEDGEMENTS

So many people have had a hand in the birth of this book. Dr Jack Hywel-Davies, Chairman of Kingsway Publications, suggested it in the first place. Miss Carrie Oates suggested the title, David Coomes, editor of Christian Weekly News-papers, has consented to the reproduction of material which first appeared in the papers which he edits. Mrs Betty Roberts has wrestled nobly with my erratic handwriting and typed the manuscript impeccably. Miss Pat Bradshaw and my wife Eira have allowed me to name them and tell the stories of their experience of Christian healing in chapter six. Dr Richard Osborne Hughes has allowed me to quote him extensively in chapter seven. Captain and Mrs Jimmy James have permitted me to refer to their experience of the ministry of deliverance in chapter ten. Mrs Jean Jordan has allowed me to tell her husband's story in chapter thirteen and fourteen. Captain Edmund Wilbourne and the Rev. Eddie Neale have permitted me to reproduce a very re-markable radio-interview in chapter fourteen. I am very grateful to them all and to many more without whom this book would not have seen the light of day – not least to all of my colleagues, church officers and parishioners who have accepted and participated in the ministry of healing so will-ingly and graciously. I thank God for them and, if they will have it, dedicate this book to them.

ROY LAWRENCE

CHAPTER ONE

The Story So Far

My first experience of Christian healing was not a conscious one at all. It happened when I was a small boy. I had been cycling round and round a friend's house on my tricycle. I took a corner too quickly and fell off on to a rockery. The result was a broken arm.

The arm was set in plaster and gradually it healed and the plaster was removed. As soon as the plaster was off I went to play in the garden of another friend, promptly fell off his swing and broke my arm again! My friend's father brought me home and broke the news to my mother.

It was obvious, I am told, that the arm was broken from the way in which it was bent at the point of the breakage, but with some considerable presence of mind my mother got me to lie between two arm chairs, with most of my body in one, my feet up on the other, and my arm held straight along a chair-arm. She held it there and kept my mind off it by telling me stories till I dropped off to sleep – and then she prayed, against all the odds, that God would heal me.

When the doctor arrived, he could see no trace of a breakage, and neither subsequently could anyone else.

I knew very little about it myself at the time except that somehow my arm had got itself better and that I would not have to go into plaster again after all. When my mother told me about it when I was older, it seemed a very odd story to me. Still I knew prayer was supposed to work. So, I concluded that perhaps it did work for some people on some occasions, and this just happened to be one of them.

And then – a long time afterwards – someone was healed through my own prayers.

When I was a student in my late teens, I was moved to lay hands on and to pray for a churchwarden who was seriously ill and apparently making no progress at all. The story is told in chapter 1 of my earlier book *Christian Healing Rediscovered*. He made a rapid and remarkable recovery.

One might expect that with those two experiences set into my consciousness, I would have been orientated towards a concern for Christian healing from the moment I felt called to the ministry. But it was not so. Somehow or other I managed to tuck both of them out of sight.

I read Classics and Theology for four years at Oxford and then went on to two further years of pre-ordination training at Cambridge. After that I embarked upon a curacy at the large, beautiful, fashionably intellectual Church of St. George's, Stockport. Had you asked me what my special interests were at that time, I would have spoken of my enthusiasm for biblical theology, for preaching, for music of various sorts, and for personal counselling. I might have mentioned my fancy for writing and broadcasting. I would certainly not have mentioned Christian healing. On the contrary I might well have recoiled from it as being academically disreputable, as smacking of superstition and mumbo-jumbo.

However, many years later I was in a car full of clergy on the way to a conference and my interest in Christian healing was rekindled in a very simple way. One of the clergy happened to say to the rest of us – 'Have you noticed that when Jesus says "Preach" to his disciples, he usually adds "and Heal"?' He said he thought it odd that the Christian church had taken one command so seriously and yet almost totally ignored the other. The conversation quickly turned to other matters, but I found that personally I had been given a 'seed-thought' which would not leave me. So as I was due to go for half a term's refresher course at Wycliffe Hall, Oxford, it seemed right to use part of the time to investigate the subject of Christian healing. By the time the refresher course was over, I had no doubts of the centrality of the concept of Christian healing to the gospel.

Healing is a primary biblical topic. In fact it is no exaggeration to say that the Bible can be described as *a book about healing*. Its concern is the healing of the total man, body, mind and spirit, the healing of relationships, the healing of society, the healing of the nations. This healing work

was the heart of the life and ministry of Jesus, and it was to
be the essence of the life and ministry of his church.

I saw too that Christian healing is by no means an illogical
concept. As doctors are increasingly telling us, body, mind
and spirit go together and affect each other. A physical condition can affect our attitude to life – as in a post-influenza
depression. Similarly our attitude to life affects our bodies.
Cherished resentment can produce various physical conditions ranging from catarrh to constipation. Anxiety can
produce a further selection ranging from skin rashes to
diarrhoea. A strong positive thought can be as physically
beneficial as a pill or medicine. No wonder people felt
physically better for meeting Jesus.

As I discussed all this with other clergy on the refresher
course, it became clear that experiences of Christian healing
were still to be found in parish life. They did not occur very
frequently in the life of the average parish. They tended to
be regarded as rather out of the ordinary when they happened. But there was hardly a clergyman to be found who
would say that he had no experience whatsoever of Christian
healing.

So scripture, logic and experience suggested that there
was a deep source of healing to be rediscovered in the name
of Christ if we were prepared to take his command seriously.
All of this raised a practical question. What did I propose
to do about Christian healing when the refresher course was
over and I was back in my parish?

What eventually happened after considerable heart-
searching and discussion with my church officers was that
with some degree of trepidation we started a service of 'investigation into Christian healing', which took place on the
first Sunday of each month, in the evening. From its beginning it proved a worthwhile service with a high quality
of worship, and after about eighteen months, healing began
to flow from it.

There is a much fuller description of all this in my earlier
book. The first four chapters include some details of the
biblical background at which I looked while at Oxford, and
particulars of the service of Christian healing in its earliest
form and of some of the healings associated with it. They

also contain an account of a mission of teaching and healing conducted for us by the Rev. George Bennett, which proved a tremendous help and encouragement to us while our own ministry of healing was in its infancy and there were many doubts and difficulties to be faced.

Eventually I felt able to change the name of our monthly service. Instead of calling it an 'investigation into Christian healing' I was able to speak of a 'rediscovery of Christian healing'. Out of sheer experience I was coming to know that healing was not just an important topic to be investigated, but a real and authentic element in the church's life, a flame of the Spirit to be rekindled, a power of the gospel to be rediscovered.

CHAPTER TWO

Starting a Christian Healing Service

In October 1975 my family and I moved to the parish of Prenton, on the outskirts of Birkenhead. Prenton is a mixed area, ranging from council estates at the perimeter to some quite large houses at the centre. There are shops, schools and sports clubs, including Tranmere Rovers Football Club. All of these are built on and around a little hill. At the top of the hill stands St. Stephen's Church, with the Church Hall and the Vicarage next to it, and half-way down the hill there is the daughter-church, St. Alban's, with a youth centre and a curacy-house next door.

It is a busy, varied parish, full of interesting possibilities and opportunities. The church folk are kindly, unobtrusive people who would not consider themselves remarkable in any way. The congregations have not for some time been remarkable for their size. And the people in the congregations are predominantly quiet and shy, in no way remarkable for their powers of evangelism. But there is one sense at least in which I believe they are truly remarkable. For the church people of Prenton, serving the Lord seems automatically to involve serving the community. They find it natural to respond in his name to the needs of those around them.

Month by month, literally hundreds of man-hours are spent by the church folk of Prenton running clubs for the elderly and play groups for toddlers and a youth centre and a sheltered housing scheme and many other caring activities. There are so many examples of this which come to mind as I write – the annual holiday for the elderly run by one of our ladies, herself a pensioner, the monthly home-made tea party for the elderly, the marathon turkey-and-trimmings dinner provided by parishioners for seventy or more lonely people on Christmas Day, the church couple who have fostered forty-eight children over the years and yet have still found time for the wife to run a play group and the husband to help at the youth centre.

I can report this without inhibition because I am in no way responsible for it. This is the way in which I found the parish. If credit is due to the clergy for it, it must go to my predecessors.

When a parish has an atmosphere of community care and concern, there are many reasons to thank God for it. One of the good things about it is that it is a natural atmosphere for a ministry of healing. Without love there can be no Christian healing. For Jesus loving and healing were inseparably intertwined, and the church which has begun to love in his name has, whether it knows it or not, already begun to do his work of healing.

So I found that I was able to begin services of Christian healing in Prenton in an unselfconscious and almost casual fashion. The church officers knew that soon after my arrival these services would begin. I had made this clear before accepting the living. But apart from that there was no fanfare of trumpets before the first Christian healing service. One evening it just happened. It seemed right to use the sermon to speak about the basic facts of Christian healing and to tell something of the story of this ministry in my former parish. At the end of the sermon I said that our Church Army Captain and I would be standing behind the communion rail during the hymn that followed and that if anyone wished to come to us we would be ready and willing to administer a laying on of hands in the name of our Lord. And forward they came – about twenty out of a small congregation of thirty or forty. The services of healing had started.

Before long a format had evolved for these services. It was similar to, though not identical with the format of the services of healing in Hyde. We started with a shortened form of Series Two evensong, reading one lesson only and using only one canticle. After trying various canticles the one we came to settle for was the little known *Salvator Mundi* which contains so many of the basic underlying truths of Christian healing.

O Saviour of the world, the Son Lord Jesus:
Stir up thy strength and help us, we humbly
     beseech thee.
By thy cross and precious blood thou hast
     redeemed us:
Save us and help us, we humbly beseech thee.
Thou didst save thy disciples when ready to perish:
Hear us and save us, we humbly beseech thee.
Let the pitifulness of thy great mercy:
Loose us from our sins, we humbly beseech thee.
Make it appear that thou art our Saviour and mighty
     Deliverer:
O save us that we may praise thee, we humbly
     beseech thee.
Draw near according to thy promise from the
     throne of thy glory:
Look down and hear our crying, we humbly
     beseech thee.
Come again and dwell with us, O Lord Christ Jesus:
Abide with us for ever, we humbly beseech thee.
And when thou shalt appear with power and great
     glory:
May we be made like unto thee in thy glorious
     kingdom.
Thanks be to thee, O Lord.
Alleluia! Amen.

The sermon, as in Hyde, soon came to consist of a Bible
study, moving chapter by chapter through Luke's gospel,
paying particular attention to the theme of healing as it
arose – and finding that it always did arise in one way or
another. We had bought copies of Luke's gospel from the
British and Foreign Bible Society. These were handed to
members of the congregation as they entered church and
collected before they left, so that all could have the text
before them as the sermon was preached. The same passage
was read as the lesson earlier in the service.

   During the hymn after the sermon a laying on of hands in
the name of Christ was made available to anyone wishing to
receive it. Anyone was free to come to the communion rail.

The invitation was put in much the same way as had become customary at Hyde – 'You are welcome to receive a laying on of hands and a prayer in the name of Christ if you wish to do so for any reason at all. Perhaps you have been ill in some way and have a need for physical healing. Perhaps you are feeling anxious or depressed and have a need for mental healing. Perhaps some temptation is hard to cope with and you are conscious of the need for spiritual healing. Or, if you wish, you may come forward just as an act of commitment, a prayer for spiritual deepening, a symbol of your availability to our Lord. Or perhaps you want to come forward as an act of prayer for someone else, whom you know to be in need of healing. Or perhaps you want to come forward simply because the touch of Christ is desirable for its own sake, quite apart from any by-products it may bring. Whatever your reasons for coming forward, you are welcome.'

Initially, two of us were behind the communion rail. Then, at subsequent services, as the number coming forward grew from twenty to thirty, forty, fifty and sixty, we increased the number of ministrants to two teams of two. First we administered a laying on of hands to each other with the prayer, 'May the healing power of the Holy Spirit be in you,' said in unison; then, two by two, we offered the same prayer and the same touch to those who came forward from the congregation.

I was fortunate that the Church Army Captain who was working in the parish before my arrival saw the point of Christian healing and agreed fully with this ministry. Soon we were joined by a curate who was also happy to involve himself in this ministry of healing. The lay readers also agreed to participate. So did a growing number of our church officers. As in Hyde, I was always happy to see a clergyman and a layman administering the laying on of hands together – the touch of Christ given by the body of Christ.

The prayers of intercession followed the laying on of hands. As the hymn finished, the congregation knelt for silent individual prayer, and as the laying on of hands finished the silent individual prayer merged into a period of corporate prayer. Then the worship ended with a hymn of praise and a blessing.

Right from the start, this service was received with thoughtfulness and graciousness in the parish – and before long it was received with positive gratefulness. I realize this does not always happen when a service of healing is introduced into the worship of a church. For instance, two parishes come to mind where the vicars have experienced difficulty in introducing a ministry of healing. In one the P.C.C. has split into two factions, a pro-charismatic and an anti-charismatic group, and the ministry of healing has become a sort of football to be kicked between the two. In another a group of local doctors have misunderstood the purpose of the ministry of Christian healing and have reacted to the Vicar with open hostility.

There have been no such traumas during the first two years of this ministry in Prenton. Just before writing this paragraph I have been out to administer a laying on of hands in the name of Christ to a local doctor, who is ill at present and who has received a ministry of Christian healing with gratitude and humility. Other local doctors have discussed the subject with me with sympathy and understanding, and some of their views will be summarized in a later chapter. The people of the church also have shown a spirit of openness which in many cases has now developed into a spirit of awareness and commitment.

Why have things worked out in this way in Prenton? Several factors seem to be involved.

I have already mentioned the 'casual' approach which now seems to be the best method of introduction. Truth is a self-validating concept. It needs no fanfare of trumpets. If there are tangible initial results, they will provide more than enough of a fanfare themselves. If there are not, then any previous fanfare would be something of an embarrassment.

The spirit of kindliness and community concern which I found already existent in Prenton has already been mentioned. This is so important. Christian healing does not happen in a vacuum. It can be actively impeded by undercurrents of bitterness and mistrust in the life of a church.

But it is nurtured and fostered by a spirit of simple practical Christian love.

There are other considerations also. I suppose there was a good deal more certainty on my part in my introduction of the ministry of healing at Prenton than there had been at Hyde. The only certainty I had in the early days at Hyde was that Christian healing is a topic of such importance and such biblical centrality that it is vital for the church to be looking at it hard and straight, researching into it, bringing thought, prayer, Bible study and the light of historical and personal experience to bear upon an honest, serious investigation, until we come to know both the facts of the matter and the nature of God's call to us. The service was an investigation, a groping towards a light which was not discerned clearly or constantly. That was the way it had to be, because we have to be honest in our approach to Christian healing or we shall damage ourselves and the Christian cause. Wishful thinking must never be a substitute for truth and experience.

However, by the time I brought this ministry to Prenton, I knew a little more of the truth and had a certain degree of experience on which to draw. Mind you, I am still very much a beginner. All that I can claim is that perhaps I have moved out of the kindergarten and into standard one in the school of Christian healing. Still, even that degree of progress brings with it an instinctive increase in authority.

I was fortunate, too, in that back in the nineteen-forties, while I was still a school-boy, a previous Vicar of Prenton had been concerned for the ministry of healing, and there is still talk of a 'miracle cure' which took place in his day. Memories of his ministry meant that Christian healing was not regarded as completely newfangled or unknown.

Also it was certainly a help that, in the early days of Christian healing services at Prenton, there were some lovely instances of healing.

One such instance concerned one of our churchwardens, a local dentist, who fell down a flight of stairs and broke five ribs. He was admitted to hospital but went on to develop double virus pneumonia. His condition deteriorated and there were fears for his life. He lay in bed with a raging temperature, absolutely soaking with the great drops of sweat which you could actually see exuding from his skin as you watched him.

I went into the hospital. We prayed together and I administered a laying on of hands in the Lord's name. It was like touching someone who had come straight out of a bath. I needed a towel to dry my hands.

Soon afterwards while I was still sitting by his bed, a nurse came with a thermometer for a routine temperature check. She took his temperature and then went off for a second thermometer. 'This one must be broken,' she explained, 'it says his temperature's normal, and it can't be.' However, it *was* normal! The second thermometer confirmed it – and a steady recovery followed.

Of course, there is no way of 'proving' that the prayers and the laying on of hands had anything to do with that recovery, but our churchwarden had no doubts about it, and subsequently he asked if he might speak to the congregation at one of our healing services. He is a shy man, not a natural talker and certainly not one to wear his heart on his sleeve. It was very moving indeed to hear him speak simply and sincerely of his experience of the touch of Christ and of his certainty that this touch had brought peace and healing where before there was turbulence and danger.

So with this help and with the co-operation and good-will of my colleagues and the other church officers, the service of Christian healing became a regular and valued part of the life of the church in Prenton.

CHAPTER THREE

Healing Prayer

In the last chapter we touched very briefly upon the prayers which follow the sermon in our service of Christian healing. These deserve more extensive consideration, partly because prayer is an essential resource of any ministry of Christian healing, and partly because there are new things to share with you here which you will not find in my earlier book.

In the early days of the healing ministry at Hyde I used to follow the practice of reading out a long list of names of people who were sick or in some sort of trouble, and sometimes I would add a description of whatever was wrong with them – 'Today our prayers are asked for Eliza Smith who has shingles, John Brown with lung cancer, little Julie Robinson whose mother has just died, George Thompson whose arthritis seems to be getting worse, Emily Jones now confined to a wheelchair with multiple sclerosis, Wally Wilkinson who has had a heart attack, Brenda Moody in hospital after a nervous breakdown . . . ' and so on, for perhaps thirty, forty or fifty names. The object, of course, was to bring to them the healing power of Christ, channelled by prayer, and there were not a few occasions when healing did in fact follow. However, there is a risk in this method of prayer. The risk is that instead of lifting the sufferers whose names we mention into the positive presence of Christ, our own minds will be filled with thoughts of their sickness and suffering and we shall end up by worrying about the destructive power of disease rather than meditating on the healing power of Christ. People could go away depressed by this sort of 'prayer', rather than uplifted by it. This was brought to my notice when attendance at the mid-week communion service where the list of the sick was read out dropped markedly for a while, because people said it made them feel so miserable.

At Hyde we found a partial solution in reading a list of names only, without any mention of symptoms or ailments, but even this could produce a rather negative effect. However, at Prenton we have, I believe, found a better way. The parish tradition is to place the prayers after the sermon and not before it as in most churches. So the prayers and not the sermon are the climax of the service. This has proved particularly fitting in our service of Christian healing. In the sermon we catch a glimpse of the healing Christ, in the laying-on-of-hands we feel his healing touch, and in the prayers we enjoy his presence and lift into that presence the needs of the world. We still have scores of individual requests for prayer. These we write in an intercession book. Of course God knows the names that are written in this book and the people to whom those names belong and the needs and problems of all those people. He knows all this much more exactly than we do. He also knows those people whose names should be in the book but have been left out because of some fault of ours or because of our ignorance. What we now do is first to recollect the presence of the risen, living, healing Christ, and then without reading a list of individual names and ailments we offer the book and its contents to God and offer our prayers as the channels of this power, love and peace. We pray that his holy and healing will may be done in body, mind and spirit, in life and in circumstance, for all those whose names are written or should be written in our book of intercession, and we thank God that we can know as we pray that his healing power is active in the world. This is a positive experience for those who are praying and good results are reported to us amongst those for whom we pray.

By a strange coincidence just as I have written the last sentence, two such results have been reported to me. The Lord has an impeccable sense of timing! First came a telephone report of an improvement in a nervous condition from a member of a nearby church, for whom we have been praying for some months. And then hard on the heels of this came a report from a member of St. Alban's, our daughter church, about a relative in America who has been suffering from 'double vision'. After inclusion on our prayer list, the condition cleared almost immediately.

News like this comes to us with increasing frequency. When we hear it we feel a tremendous sense of privilege. When a church embarks upon a serious ministry of Christian healing, it seems that this ministry reaches out not just to people who are present in church but to people who have never attended our services and who may live many miles away.

A lady comes to mind – let's call her Agatha – who phoned me up a year ago from her home in North Wales. She was suffering from dangerously high blood pressure. No treatment seemed to bring it down. Her doctor was worried. She was worried, and the more she worried the worse her condition became. Then she came across my book *Christian Healing Rediscovered* and telephoned to tell me about her high blood pressure and to ask for prayer. I promised to include her on our intercession list. Three months later she phoned to say that her condition was no longer critical. The pills she was taking seemed at last to be working. In a further three months she phoned again to say that the improvement had continued and that the medical treatment had been reduced.

Of course, it can never be proved that this and other instances are not coincidental. All I can do is to repeat William Temple's dictum – 'I find that when I pray coincidences happen. When I stop praying, coincidences stop happening.'

So far this chapter has dealt with general principles. I want to turn now to something more specific and detailed – a method of healing prayer, which we use from time to time at our Christian healing service, and which can also be used privately. I call it 'the ring of peace'. Various people have told me that they find it an effective method of prayer. Try it and see for yourself.

1. Begin by recollecting the presence of Christ. If you are praying within a group your group has the promise of Jesus – 'Where two or three are gathered together in my name, there am I in the midst' (Matthew 18:20). If you are in private prayer, he is still with you. You have his

word – 'I am with you always, even to the end of the world.' (Matthew 28:20.)

2. So there you are, you and Jesus. What sort of experience is it to be in his presence? He has not changed, 'He is the same yesterday, today and for ever' (Hebrews 13:8). He is the same Jesus who 'went about preaching the gospel of the kingdom and healing all manner of sickness and disease among the people' (Matthew 4:23). He is the same Jesus who promised his disciples, 'Peace I leave with you; my peace I give to you.' (John 14:27.) If we are available to him, open to him as Saviour and Lord, not fighting him but prepared for him to have his way with us, then we are within the healing peace of God which Jesus came to bring to us.

3. There is a common error concerning the peace of God. We tend to think of it as something rather precarious which we have to strive hard to hold and keep or else it will slip away, whereas the biblical picture is precisely the opposite. 'The peace of God, which passes all under-standing, will keep your hearts and minds through Christ Jesus.' (Philippians 4:7.) We do not keep the peace of God. The peace of God keeps us. So the mental picture which I suggest for this meditation is that of yourself surrounded by the ring of God's peace. There is no need to strive. Just rest in the knowledge that it is so.

4. There is another common error which thinks of the peace of God as a weak and passive concept. But the peace of God is no mere absence of turmoil. It is strong and active and vibrant with life. It must be so because it is an attribute of God himself. A common title of God in the New Testament is 'the God of peace'. The peace of God is one with the power of God, and the love of God, and the joy of God. To be within God's ring of peace is to be in contact with God's power and love and joy. It is a place of creativity, a place of healing.

5. So there is no need to do anything. Just 'go flop' before the

Lord. Acknowledge his peace. Enjoy his peace. Let his
peace flow round you. Let his peace flow into you – warm,
strong and life-giving. There is no hurry. You can rest in
this place of healing as long as you choose to do so. You
can actually feel the peace of God entering into every part
of your mind, every part of your body, the very depths of
your spirit. You can know that sin and tension and sickness
must retreat before it.

6. When the time is right, bring others into the ring of
   peace. Picture your family within the ring of peace. Lift
   up each member into that peace. Thank God that it is his
   will that your home should be a place of his peace and that
   peace should undergird all the relationships of family life,
   and as you thank God, offer your prayer as the instrument
   and vehicle of his will. Then bring into the ring of peace
   any known to you who are ill or in trouble. In each case
   do not concentrate on the illness or the trouble. Think of
   each one as a person created and loved by God, a person
   for whom God's will is wholeness. Let your prayer re-
   inforce God's will as you picture yourself and the one for
   whom you are praying within the ring of peace. Again, do
   not strive or worry or tense up. Let God's own peace do
   God's own work.

7. In our service of healing, we imagine the ring of peace
   growing larger and larger. After picturing our individual
   selves within the ring of God's peace, we encircle the
   whole congregation, all of us in church – our families too
   – with that same ring of peace. We thank God for each
   other. We thank God for himself in our midst. We thank
   God that his presence and his peace are not passive, but
   actively at work in that moment, full of purpose and
   power. Then we bring within the ring of peace all those
   for whom we have been asked to pray, all those whose
   names are, or should be, in our intercession book. We read
   no list of names and ailments, but simply align our prayers
   with God's holy and healing will, offering ourselves as
   channels of that will for peace and wholeness. As a symbol
   of this prayer, I usually lift and hold the intercession book

as we pray. Then we picture the ring of peace around our neighbourhood, then around our country, then encircling our world, and finally surrounding the whole universe known and unknown. 'Thy holy and healing will be done,' we pray, and we thank God that we can offer this prayer with confidence. The will of the almighty and eternal God must ultimately triumph, his peace must prevail, his kingdom will come – because he is God. So these are strong prayers, not weak prayers. We can offer them not with anxiety but with calm expectancy.

There are many other methods of healing prayer, but it might well prove indigestible to describe more than one at a time, and I do hope that you will actually put this book down at the end of this chapter and rest awhile within the ring of peace yourself, going through the stages one by one without hurrying.

There have been a number of occasions when I have been grateful to do this myself. Recently I had to attend a BBC Morning Service Course at the Churches' TV and Radio Centre at Bushey, near Watford. It was clearly going to be an exacting course, and I could learn a great deal from it. The trouble was that I had just started with what promised to be a nasty cold. My nose was blocked, my throat was sore and by any normal prognosis things would get worse. I decided that I had to put the journey along the motorway from Birkenhead to Bushey to good use by spending that time in healing prayer. So for three hours or so I alternated the ring of peace sequence of prayer with a meditation on the work of the Holy Spirit, which will be described later in this book. This improved my driving, if anything, because one's mind is never less clear or less efficient for practising the presence of God. And the cold? I could feel it ebbing away round about Birmingham. By the time I reached Bushey there was not a trace of it. Nor was there any trace of it during the course or after it. I find it very difficult to attribute this sequence of events to coincidence. For a clergyman I have a well developed capacity for doubt and scepticism, but so often tangible results follow healing prayer. See for yourself. The ring of God's peace is waiting for you.

CHAPTER FOUR

More Problems

Dr Leslie Weatherhead once said to a congregation of Oxford students that if there were any present who had no problems connected with the faith, they should see him in the vestry afterwards – and he would be happy to give them a few!

Certainly as far as Christian healing is concerned my own experience is that involvement in this ministry brings a confrontation with a wide variety of problems. In my former book I tried to grapple with some of them – why does Christian healing seem sometimes to 'work' and sometimes 'not work' at a physical level? Why when two men are prayed for and ministered to in an identical fashion does one live and the other one die? Why is pain and disease permitted to exist at all, if this world is the creation of a loving God? What is the relationship between the medical approach to healing and the spiritual approach? Is there a conflict between the two?

It would be nice to be able to report that as the years have gone by in this ministry, the difficulties have resolved themselves and unquestioning certainty now prevails. However, what seems to happen is that as I glean scraps of new wisdom, simultaneously I become aware of new questions which must be asked, new problems which must be faced.

So the only honest way I know of writing this second book on Christian healing involves looking again at some of the old problems and raising new ones as well. If I should make you aware of difficulties which you have never thought of before – then I offer my sincere apologies to you. Still I believe they would be bound to rear their ugly heads sooner or later for anyone who embarks on a serious study of Christian healing, so perhaps it is better to be shown them by a friend than to suffer the shock of just stumbling upon them.

One worry which some people have about the ministry of Christian healing is that they are afraid that it may be basically an emotional phenomenon. If it were so it could be a frothy, shallow thing and there might be undesirable after-effects. However, it cannot too often be said that Christian healing is *not* basically an emotional phenomenon. Some Christian healing services are more emotional than others, and indeed there must be a place for the emotions in worship because God wants worship to be an offering of our total selves, including our emotions. Also any real acceptance of the liberating power of the gospel cannot be other than a warming and joyful experience. But the root of Christian healing is not emotional. It is nothing more and nothing less than an encounter with Jesus Christ. For this we need a clear head and a clear vision. The mind and the spirit work together to perceive the reality of Jesus. An act of will makes us receptive to him. And so the healing resources of the Holy Trinity, Father, Son and Spirit, are activated around us and in us.

Our own services at St. Stephen's are notably unemotional. People who come expecting 'fireworks' of some kind are sometimes surprised how calm and matter-of-fact everything is. There is a sense of need, and of expectancy, and of the presence of the Holy Spirit, but all within a quiet thoughtful atmosphere more reminiscent of Holy Communion than anything else.

Another difficulty which some people have about Christian healing was put to me only recently in my study by a young ordinand. 'Is there not a risk,' he said, 'that a healing service may actually destroy somebody's faith if he comes to church believing that he or someone close to him will be healed and then nothing happens?'

I was very conscious of this risk during my early days in the ministry of healing. All I can say is that so far honestly I know of *no instance at all* in which any person has been damaged spiritually, mentally or physically through attending one of our services of healing. Any G.P. would be proud if he could make that claim about his surgery! Very fre-

quently one or two, or three or even half a dozen people
will telephone, write, or call at the Vicarage during the
month which follows each healing service to say thāt they
have been healed or helped in some way either by the service
immediately past or at a former service, but as I write this
chapter I am not able to tell you a single story of anyone who
has been harmed at one of them.

So far as my own experience goes, it is usual for faith to
be undiminished even when the ministry of healing is not
followed by a physical cure. In fact paradoxically under
these circumstances faith is sometimes strangely strengthened.
For instance in chapter twelve of my earlier book on healing
the story was told of 'Dora', a deeply committed Christian
woman who developed what proved to be a terminal cancer.
Her husband, her son and her daughter-in-law were non-
churchgoers. Her husband on more than one occasion voiced
his scepticism as a neighbouring minister and I administered
a laying on of hands and prayed for Dora's healing. Though
she told me that the laying on of hands often brought a
period of freedom from pain, physical healing did not follow.
Her death saddened the whole church, the whole neighbourhood. But then something very curious happened. Her husband, her son and her daughter-in-law started to come to
church. One might have expected that their scepticism would
have been reinforced, but unaccountably they found themselves at this point with the glimmerings of faith. Dora's
husband attended church until his own death. Their son and
his wife still attend thoughtfully and steadily.

Another problem perhaps follows naturally at this point.
The new found faith of Dora's family seems to be surviving
the test of time. But what about the general application of
the test of time when applied to the overall effect of the
ministry of Christian healing on the bodies, minds and
spirits of those who receive it? Do the benefits of this ministry
last? Or is there any justification in the fear that some people
have that the short-term uplift of this ministry may be
followed by long-term let-down.

I believe there is no reason at all why there should be any
long-term ill effects. If I am right in saying that Christian
healing is not an emotional phenomenon, then it is not

logical to expect an initial euphoria followed by a long-term disappointment. On the contrary. If Christian healing brings a strong and true positive influence into a troubled life and this manifests itself by an increase of health in body, mind or spirit today, then what is true and helpful today will be true and helpful tomorrow. Its application tomorrow will bring a further benefit. In other words Christian healing is not a 'magic moment' or a 'flash in the pan'; it is a way of life, and for those who continue in it the benefits ought to be cumulative rather than diminishing.

It is lovely to see that this is often the way in which it has worked out in the case of people whose stories were told in my earlier book.

'Sarah' comes to mind. Her story went like this.

One of the congregation had a heart incident. Her doctor told her that she should give up smoking, but when I visited her she said that she was incapable of doing so. She said she was a slave to cigarettes. As she lay in bed, there was an open packet of cigarettes on the bedside table. She said she just had to have it there within easy reach. I said to her, 'Let's see what the Lord can do about it.' There and then we prayed together, not specifically about the cigarettes, but about the goodness and power and love of Christ. In his name I administered a laying on of hands. A fortnight later I met her leaning on her gate. 'You'll never believe it,' she said. 'I haven't had a single cigarette since you visited me. I just haven't wanted to.' Since then she has not smoked. The urge has gone.

Now looking back at this incident four years later, I am able to report that not only has Sarah been able to remain a non-smoker but that she has had no recurrence of the heart trouble, even though during those four years she has had the physical and mental strain of nursing a sister terminally ill with cancer.

I think also of the remarkable story of 'Melanie'. All I was able to write in my previous book was –

At our mission of teaching and healing a young wife came forward for a laying on of hands. She was a keen Christian but bitter because she was suffering from multiple sclerosis. Afterwards, the multiple sclerosis seemed untouched but the bitterness had gone. It would be wrong to say that there was no healing.

I knew the bitterness had gone because Melanie came to the Vicarage for a subsequent counselling session and a further laying on of hands and it was a lovely and moving experience to see the Spirit of Christ liberated and shining in her. But at that stage her body was far from liberated. Poor girl, her walk was a slow painful shuffle, and often even this was too much for her and she had to use a wheel-chair. Everybody knew that unless there was a miracle the only future she could expect was that of progressive deterioration. Somebody said to me 'When I see Melanie walk – then I'll believe in Christian healing!'

The time soon came for me to leave the parish and with it I left Melanie. The months went by, a year passed, two years passed – and then something quite extraordinary happened. I had been invited to speak to a group of social workers in Manchester about Christian healing, and while we were having a cup of tea together one of them started talking about Melanie. It seemed he knew her and her husband well. Gradually and incredibly it dawned on me as he described Melanie's present life that he was talking about someone who was *completely whole*! As soon as I was back at the Vicarage I telephoned Melanie's home and heard the whole story from her.

Some months after she received our ministry of Christian healing she became aware of small improvements in her condition. Within a year the hospital she attended as an outpatient noticed the improvement too. She was told she was 'going into remission' and physiotherapy was prescribed to help her make the most of it. Gradually it became clear that this was much more than a remission. The improvement continued. Melanie got out of her wheel-chair and back on to two sticks, and then found she could manage with one stick, and then that she did not need a stick at all. She was able to walk – and walk normally. She went hiking! She played tennis! After eleven years off work she started work again. The hospital stopped her treatment and told her she could no longer be said to have multiple sclerosis. All the side-effects disappeared. Beforehand she suffered from double vision. This has now become normal. Beforehand her speech was slurred. Now it is crystal-clear.

A few months ago I visited Melanie in her home and watched her bustling about the house making me a cup of tea, preparing her husband's meal, coping with the family hubbub. She told me that though she was very grateful for all that the doctors, nurses and physiotherapists had done for her, she has no doubt at all that her present wholeness is due to the power of God activated by the ministry of Christian healing. I also saw the final touch to that healing. Her formerly scrawny legs had filled up again and become shapely and feminine. The Lord had not done things for her by halves!

This story and the earlier story of 'Dora' lead to one further question. What should be our attitude to so-called 'incurable' conditions? Dora had an 'incurable' condition, and as it turned out there was no cure for her in this life. But Melanie also had an 'incurable' condition – and now she is brimming with health and wholeness.

My feeling is that we should abandon the word 'incurable'. Medically it is of dubious value and its application changes from year to year. Many of the diseases which would have been on the list of incurable conditions fifty years ago are no longer on it. Fifty years from now many of the diseases on today's list of incurable conditions will no longer be on it. Theologically the word is of less value still. God is not bound to a list made fifty years ago, or today, or fifty years ahead. The rigidity of thought which a word like 'incurable' can engender needs to be put aside gently but firmly as we open ourselves to the healing love of God and realize that the potentialities of that healing love are as infinite as he is himself.

CHAPTER FIVE

Two Items of Unfinished Business

Sometimes in discussing the problems raised by a ministry of Christian healing one can speak of them in a detached and academic way. Sometimes, however, the problems are more personal.

While I was writing *Christian Healing Rediscovered* there were two such problems which caused me considerable heartache and which from time to time made me wonder whether to abandon the book completely. When the book was finished, the problems were still worrying items of 'unfinished business'.

At the start of that book there is a list of acknowledgements to people who played an essential part in its production. Prominent amongst them were Pat Bradshaw, who as the preface said 'as an act of Christian stewardship served as my secretary at St. George's, Hyde, and typed the manuscript of this book,' and my wife Eira, whom I thanked because she 'not only patiently bore the preoccupied neglect which writers tend to heap upon their marriage-partners but also made many helpful comments out of her experience as a physiotherapist'. What I did not add was that both were in need of physical healing and that no healing seemed to be forthcoming.

Pat's trouble was one which was causing her considerable worry and which was beginning to threaten her secretarial career with a local firm. A little bony lump had developed on her right-hand just above the palm at the base of the index finger. Initially it was smaller than a pea but it was inconvenient and uncomfortable and soon it started to interfere with her work. Periodically Pat received a laying-on-of-hands at our Christian healing services. Each time the lump seemed to grow a little! Sometimes I asked her to be one of the team administering the laying on of hands at the communion rail and so she laid hands on others and occupied a real place in the healing ministry of the church. But there seemed to be no healing for Pat and her doctor said that an operation might be necessary. She soldiered on both as a recipient and as a ministrant in our ministry of healing, sometimes going as part of a group to other parishes which wanted to know about our ministry, occasionally speaking at meetings and conferences on the subject. But her lump seemed singularly unimpressed by any of it.

Stoically she finished typing the manuscript of my book on healing and we shared the leadership at a Church Army conference on healing in London, but as I left the parish of St. George's, Hyde, I went with the sadness of knowing that Pat's problem was still a worry and a threat to her. I believed all I had written, and yet I felt so ineffective. Faith was supposed to move mountains so surely Pat's lump could not be beyond its influence!

Some months after my family and I had moved to our new parish, Pat was again asked to take part in the leadership of a Church Army conference on Christian healing. It was to be held in Folkestone and with her were to go a former curate of St. George's and one of the church officers. Pat's lump was now more than a year old and had grown to the size of a marble and nobody could have blamed her if she had decided that Christian healing was not her scene, but nonetheless she went to Folkestone and spoke again of her conviction that God is calling today's church to a ministry of healing. At question time one of the members of the conference asked her directly whether she had any personal experience of Christian healing in her own body, and she had to admit that though she believed that her personality had benefited from the healing touch of our Lord she could claim no experience of personal physical healing whatsoever. A service of healing ended the conference. Pat's hand and Pat's lump were laid on the heads of the conference members and everyone went home.

On the train back north a steward came into Pat's compartment and asked if she would like to have some coffee. Pat thanked him, took her gloves off and found quite unexpectedly that her lump had vanished without trace! The healing we had hoped for had come at last. It was instantaneous and complete. She came to Birkenhead to visit us soon after and we were able to see for ourselves that her hand was perfect. It still is so, as I write these words two years later.

Why did Pat have to wait for her healing? Why did it happen in that way at that moment? Why was her faith tested for so many months? I wish I knew.

Pat's lump was not the only item of unfinished business in our ministry of healing at that time. My wife Eira was undergoing an experience which was in some ways similar during our closing years in Hyde. Before we married, whilst Eira was working as a physiotherapist, she had slipped a disc when lifting an eighteen-stone patient. She was off work and in bed for a while, and when she started work again she was aware of a weakness in her back and of the need to take care.

This weakness was still with her when we married, and it constituted a real problem for her, because being the wife of a Vicar is a much more strenuous business than most people realize. For a start there is a large house to care for, and usually a large garden thrown in for good measure. Literally hundreds of people have to be entertained during the course of each year. Scores of cups of tea and coffee are brewed for callers who range from visiting bishops to visiting tramps. Sometimes the church's guests have to be entertained overnight or for a longer period. When the church, or the church hall, needs spring-cleaning it falls to the Vicar's wife to lead the bucket-and-mop brigade. The Vicarage phone and door bell ring with frightening frequency. The call could be someone wanting to demonstrate a new product for cleaning the church floor. It could be someone wanting to arrange a christening, or a wedding, or a funeral. It could be a couple with a marriage problem or someone feeling suicidal, who decides to try religion as a last resort before putting his head in a gas oven. On such occasions the odds are that I will be out at a service or a meeting or that I will be out visiting in the parish. So whatever the problem is, more often than not, Eira is landed with it. And simultaneously of course

the life of the family has to go on. Being a wife and mother
with an unpredictable husband and two energetic lads to
look after is a demanding occupation in itself. I remember
the day when one of our boys was sick in the hall just as the
Bishop arrived for dinner. I remember the fortnight when
I was away as Chaplain at a Territorial Army class, bliss-
fully unaware that the day after I left Eira and both boys
went down with mumps. And I shall never forget an incredible day when I was in bed with 'flu. Eira had fallen
awkwardly in the drive and hurt both legs, but one of our
boys had to be packed up and sent off to his boarding school
because it was the first day of his second term there; and
still the phone bell and the door bell worked overtime, and
our callers included an Italian tourist in need of companion-
ship and a man who had just seen *The Exorcist* and thought
he was devil-possessed!

We are sometimes told that our Vicarage has an atmosphere of peace and tranquillity. A miracle in itself! But after
a while it became clear that the peace and tranquillity which
others found was taking its toll on Eira. Whilst we were at
Hyde her back began to give renewed trouble and year after
year the problem increased. She had to have days in bed,
then a week, then a fortnight. Often her movements were
stiff and painful and she said that she felt ninety-nine years
old. A check X-ray showed continued narrowing of the disc
spaces – but seeing the trouble was one thing, healing it was
another.

In vain she tried the various exercises on herself which
she knew so well as a physiotherapist. In vain we prayed for
her healing and I administered a laying on of hands in the
Lord's name both in church and at home. In theory Eira
believed in Christian healing. It made sense to her as a
physiotherapist and as a Christian. But in practice she grew
steadily worse and she began to fear she might turn into a
permanent invalid. Yet all this time the production of my
first book on healing was proceeding with Eira's full support
and encouragement.

Then we were asked to move from Hyde to Birkenhead,
and our hearts failed us when we saw what was to be our
next Vicarage. Hyde Vicarage was reasonably large but it

paled into insignificance beside Prenton Vicarage. Ten bed-rooms! Twenty-eight rooms altogether! What a load to put on Eira's creaking back. The church council was marvellous and as an act of faith authorized the spending of thousands of pounds, which they did not have, on modernizing and improving the house as far as possible. We believed it was the place where God wanted us to be, but Eira was not a little afraid as we moved in. She prayed: 'Lord, it all seems impossible to me. I don't see how I can cope at all. If you are calling us to this new work, *you* will have to cope for me.'

Praise be, he did just that! Some months after our arrival in Prenton just about at the same time as Pat's 'unfinished business' was being cleared up, the Lord gave Eira's back the same treatment as Pat's lump. One Sunday evening after our monthly service of Christian healing, as Eira was having a bath, quite suddenly she knew she was healed. She stepped out of the bath and for the first time in eighteen years she touched her toes. Her first impulse was to weep. She felt certain she was healed. And yet supposing it was some cruel delusion? What would happen to her faith? What would happen to her sanity? Because of her mixture of feelings she said nothing to me for some weeks, but in due course she told me that she believed herself to be healed and so it proved to be.

The difference in her now is most remarkable. For years I had carried the tea-tray from the kitchen to the sitting room because it hurt Eira's back. Suddenly she was able to carry it herself without trouble. If anything life has become more exacting than ever for her, but she finds she can put her new back into it without harm. On the occasions when we have spent afternoons together cleaning up our massive garden, I am the one who has collected any back-aches that were going, not Eira. She has a degree of supple movement now that I have never known in her before. On the very day that this chapter has been written, we have been visiting a submarine at Birkenhead docks. Eira has been climbing up and down the conning-tower and squeezing in and out of the narrow hatches. Three years ago it would have been quite impossible. Today there was no problem at all.

Again one wonders why the healing was delayed and why

faith was tested. One idea which I was taught when I was a child was that God always answers prayer, but that the answer can come in three ways, sometimes 'Yes', sometimes 'No' and sometimes 'Wait'. If that is so Pat and Eira fit decidedly into the third category. But I am sure that this is an over-simplification and that many factors other than the will of God are involved in those cases where healing is delayed or denied. Perhaps one day we shall understand these things. In the meantime all we can do is to carry on taking our Father's love on trust from Jesus and this will ensure that when God's healing moment comes we are ready, willing and available.

CHAPTER SIX

Medical Reactions

It would be quite wrong to regard me as a specialist in Christian healing. I have no psychic gift, no specialist experience, no sense of calling to be a 'healer' beyond the fact that I am a parson working in a parish and it seems to me that Christian healing is a basic ingredient of ordinary parish ministry.

Still I suppose the fact that the ministry of Christian healing has been neglected in the church for so many years means that any clergyman who takes it at all seriously finds himself a jump or two ahead of the church as a whole. 'In the kingdom of the blind the one-eyed man is king!'

So it is that with increasing frequency I find myself invited to speak at meetings or services or clergy conferences on the subject of Christian healing. Some months ago I was privileged to be a speaker at a conference for close on two hundred doctors, nurses, clergy and social workers organized as part of the doctors' in-service training at Prestwich Hospital Regional Conference Centre, Manchester.

The conference title was 'Curing and Caring' and the subject I was asked to speak on was 'The Spiritual Dimension of Healing'. Sandwiched as I was between lectures by two senior consultants, it was with no little trepidation that I finally found myself on my feet before the conference. The conference secretary had warned me that I could not take it for granted that everyone present was a 'believer'. All that could be taken for granted was that everyone present had a real concern for some aspect of healing.

I cannot remember exactly what I said, because I tend not to work from a script on these occasions, but it was something like this . . .

'Some of you may be afraid that by comparison with the

medical exactitudes you can expect from the doctors who are speaking here today, my contribution may be distinctly amateurish and even disreputable. If it is so the fault will be mine and not that of my subject, because Christian healing, as I understand it, does not conflict with any man's professional or intellectual integrity. There is no "mumbo-jumbo" about it. It is not a venture into the occult. It certainly goes far beyond my powers of understanding, but so far as I do understand it I do not find that my faith and my reason are in any sort of conflict.

'Man is a complex entity, a combination of body, mind and that illusive essence of personality which is sometimes called the spirit. These elements are interdependent. They all affect each other. The body affects the spirit, as in a post-'flu or post-natal depression. The spirit affects the body, as in a skin condition brought on by anxiety. So since we cannot disentangle the body from the spirit, there must be a spiritual dimension in healing.

'Or look at it another way. It is sometimes said that there is a mysterious "X-factor" in healing. I remember a wise doctor once saying to me, "I cannot heal anybody. All I can do is to try to create the optimum condition for the body to heal itself." There is a demonstrable force at work in the world which shows itself in creation and, where there is damage, shows itself in re-creation or healing. If I break my arm, the bones knit together. If I cut myself whilst shaving, the cut heals. The healing force which makes this happen is not created medically, it is a given ingredient in life as we know it.

'However, though this is a given ingredient, it is not given equally on all occasions. Sometimes the healing force flows vigorously. Sometimes it flows sluggishly. The question for all those who have a concern for healing is "How can we increase its vigour?" Clearly there are medical ways, but there are also non-medical ways. I remember talking to a doctor who told me that as quite a junior G.P. he had learned the importance of an element in healing which was not strictly medical. He was called to the bedside of a poorly old lady whom he knew well and who trusted and respected him completely. As he entered the room she said, "I shall feel better now, doctor," and as he sat by her bedside holding her hand her racing pulse slowed down under his fingers until it became absolutely normal. He realized at that point that there was no medical reason for the improvement in the condition which was taking place before his eyes and under his hands. He said to me that he knew in that moment that there was more to healing than pills and a stethoscope.

'Jesus had a healing effect upon people in a way that was perhaps similar in nature to this, though much greater in degree. Healing the sick was an integral and basic element in his life and ministry, and he commanded his followers to involve themselves in the same healing ministry.'

I added three illustrations of the way in which this ministry of healing can be operative today. First I read the story of 'Greg' from chapter 10 of *Christian Healing Rediscovered*, a man whose mind was made heavy and whose body was made sick by suppressed anger, but who found liberation from his anger and its mental and physical consequences in an encounter with Christ. Here the psycho-dynamics of what was happening were not too hard to see. Then I told them the story of 'Melanie', in much the same way as in chapter 4 in the present book, and saw a few brows wrinkle in puzzlement, because there the psycho-somatic element is more difficult to discern. Then, to show that though Christian healing is not anti-rational it does go immeasurably further than our powers of reasoning can at present take us, I ended with the startling incident of 'raising the dead' which comes later in this book, illustrating it with a tape recording of the man who had been 'dead' but was now alive.

My talk had lasted about half an hour. When it finished, the questions and comments came thick and fast, and when we paused for lunch they still kept coming, and they were noticeably courteous, appreciative and discerning in their nature. It was good to be there and encouraging to be taken so seriously. Dozens of copies of my book were bought.

Subsequently I talked to another doctor about this experience. He, though himself an agnostic, was not at all surprised. He said that most good doctors are taking an increasingly holistic approach to their healing work, tending the whole person rather than some limb or organ in isolation. He seemed to think that it was a decided improvement on past performance if the church too was now concerning itself with the whole person rather than isolating 'spiritual matters' from the whole life of the whole man.

There are many encouraging features in my relationships with doctors these days. I think of the Middlesex G.P. who wrote to ask me to pray for the patients in his practice and said that he is making it his aim to combine his general medical practice with some measure of spiritual counselling. I think of the Yorkshire parish where I was asked to talk to a large group of members of the church and found that their ministry of Christian healing was being jointly led by the Vicar and a local doctor.

I think too of my own parish, because a large number of doctors live in our neighbourhood. None of them has so far expressed to me any hostile feelings in connection with our church's ministry of Christian healing, and some give me active encouragement.

Recently one of them, Dr Richard Osborne Hughes, a consultant in general and geriatric medicine at one of our local hospitals, invited me to his home to discuss the contents of my first book. I took my tape recorder and with his permission recorded the discussion. He has kindly said that I may reproduce some of his comments here.

He began by saying that he believed that any doctor who took a purely 'mechanistic' approach to his work misses a vital dimension of his work. A mechanistic approach is perhaps understandable in these days of kidney-machines and heart transplants and powerful drugs, but to confine oneself to it is to opt out of the work of healing seen as a whole. He felt that my book had been a healthy corrective to this danger.

'I felt,' he said, 'on reading through your book that it would be very helpful if a lot of doctors would read it, because it might well give them more insight into human nature. In going through the book I found myself again and again putting comments in the margin such as "Absolutely", "Agree", and "Yes", where you have precisely hit the nail on the head. This is mainly in connection with psychological problems, which I feel provide the major opportunities for invoking faith either in a person or in an All-powerful Being. However, there are probably no medical conditions at all which are completely without a psychological element. For example, consider the case of a broken leg, which one would naturally regard as something relatively mechanistic. As far as the knitting of the bone afterwards is concerned, and the recovery of the muscle power, and the return of the person towards normality, it is common knowledge in the medical profession that the impact of a broken leg will be less for instance on an amateur sportsman who is playing for pleasure than on a professional whose living depends on it. The less psychological stress there is the less trouble there is likely to be in the healing process.

'Perhaps I am too restrictive in talking about "psychological" problems and "psychological" answers to them, and you are nearer the truth when you speak about "faith". One of our problems today is that an increasing number of people seem to be lacking any sort of faith. Not only do they lack faith in God but they tend to lack faith in anything – faith in their country, faith in any political party, faith in church, faith in a local football team, and worst of all, faith in themselves. As part of this general lack of faith, there comes a loss of faith in one's own powers of recovery when sick. The little setbacks which occur during the course of recovery assume a quite disproportionate importance, and the lack of faith becomes a positive barrier to getting better.

'Faith seems to provide the key to the management of life. People with faith lead a much happier life than those without it. And faith seems also to provide the key to the management of death.

'When people come to see a doctor the weakening of faith is often an imortant element in the condition they bring. They don't just come with a symptom, but because they are frightened or worried or puzzled about their symptom. Hopefully they have faith in their doctor and this helps him restore their faith in life. In the same way if they come to a clergyman with faith in him, they are already on the way to improvement. If they come to him within the context of a church service of healing, the quietness, the withdrawal from the world's hubbub and the act of focusing the mind on that which is outside oneself all add to the occasion's potential for healing.

'I sometimes talk about an "X-factor" which is difficult to pinpoint medically but which is absolutely essential for the healing process. I am sure it is connected with faith. Also, since reading your book, I feel it must be connected with what you call the Holy Spirit.'

Dr Osborne Hughes questioned me fairly closely about what I meant by the Holy Spirit, and as I described the nature and workings of the Holy Spirit, the inner Godhead to which we are called by our Father through Jesus Christ, he became increasingly convinced that we were coming to the heart of the healing process.

'There seem to be two principal fears in the lives of many people,' he said, 'the fear of death and the fear of going mad. It seems that a sense of the Holy Spirit can combat both of these, by providing a strong sense of our own identity and a strong optimism that we can live until we die (and perhaps after we die) and that, in consequence, we can discard worry and depression and negativity. I take it that one of the results of prayer and of thoughtful church-going is to recharge our "positivity batteries" by strengthening our sense of the Holy Spirit.

'In that Jesus stirs the Holy Spirit, I think it could be said that he is the ultimate psychiatrist. One of the reasons why I think your book is worthwhile for doctors to read is that it must be good for a doctor to think about the force which you call 'the Holy Spirit' as a resource for healing. I suppose that both you clergy and we doctors are dealing with this force, but it seems to me that in dealing with it the tools of your trade are superior to ours. Your therapeutic armamentarium is far better than anything we've got!

'I think it is high time that doctors as well as clergy realized that if we human beings become increasingly heathen and give in to the pressures which are around us and allow our faith to be weakened and our spirit to be sapped – then we are on course for sickness and all the tablets in the world are not going to make us better!'

It was a significant statement, I thought, and worth quot-

ing at length – though of course I have no way of knowing
how representative views such as these are of the medical
profession as a whole. It was midnight before we stopped
talking. We had ranged over all sorts of elements in the life
of a doctor and the life of a vicar and had seen that they
have a great deal in common. It seemed a long time ago
since the first services of Christian healing at St. George's,
Hyde, and the real suspicion with which they were regarded
by some of the local doctors. Perhaps I am luckier these
days. Perhaps I am learning to express myself rather better.
Perhaps there is an actual development in medical thinking
which brings doctors closer to the spiritual dimension in
healing.

In any event I am more convinced than ever that there
is no basic conflict between medical practice and Christian
healing, and that the more contact and communication
there is between those involved in both callings the better
it will be for the Health Service and for the churches and
for all those who stand in need of healing.

CHAPTER SEVEN

'By His Wounds We Are Healed'

There are two principal ways of coming into a ministry of Christian healing. There are those who become aware that they have a gift of healing and resolve that they must offer it to the Lord. This was the basis of the ministry of healing in the Somerset parish of Moorlinch, which is described in the fourth appendix of my earlier book. Two ladies offered their gifts of healing to the local church and in due course the Vicar discovered that he had a similar gift. On the other hand there are others who have no sort of awareness of a gift of healing but who embark upon this ministry in simple obedience to our Lord's command that his church should exercise a healing ministry just as he did himself. (Luke 9:1–2, 6; Luke 10:1–9; etc.) Any necessary 'gifts' they leave to the Lord's own provision.

I have come into the ministry of healing in this latter way, and am grateful that it has been so for two reasons. First the fact that I am not aware of any special personal gift of healing means that anyone who believes in the power of Jesus to bring wholeness to our sick world can do whatever I can do. If I had some strange and remarkable psychic force flowing through me, it might be very impressive, but Mr and Mrs Average Believer would have difficulty in identifying themselves with me. It is precisely because I am an ordinary vicar of an ordinary church with no awareness of extra-ordinary gifts or talents in the ministry of healing that I know I can invite *you* to share in this ministry.

Secondly, if I had some psychic gift to offer to the Lord I might sometimes be tempted to rely on *it* rather than on *him*, whereas the essence of Christian healing whether or not the ministrant is aware of a personal gift must lie in a living encounter with the living Christ. I always dislike it if anyone

47

refers to me as a 'healer', because in the way in which I see
Christian healing there is only one healer, and that healer
is Jesus.

This surely is how it must be, because Christian healing is
concerned not merely with physical cures but with wholeness
of the entire man or, in other words, with salvation. In our
English New Testament the Greek words *sozo* and *diasozo*
are translated either as 'save' (94 times) or as 'heal' (16
times) according to context. Salvation and healing are inseparably interrelated. So if the gospel of salvation is being
truly communicated we should expect to see in the lives of
those who receive it a movement towards wholeness of body,
mind and spirit. When the saving power of Jesus was
doubted, it was natural for him to say – 'But look around
you at the evidence. The blind receive their sight. The
lame walk. The lepers are cleansed. The deaf hear. The
dead are raised up!' (Matthew 11:4–5.) On the other hand
we should expect equally that any true ministry of Christian
healing will involve the communication of the simplicities of
the gospel. The two concepts are as inseparable as two sides
of a coin. If anyone claims to practise Christian healing but
does not overtly point to the saving power of Jesus Christ,
his ministry is at best partial and at worst false.

If this is true, it has many implications. Above all it brings
us to consider an element in Christian healing which is
absolutely unique and which clearly distinguishes 'Christian'
healing from any other sort of healing. The supreme paradox
and the supreme mystery of the Christian faith is that it is
only as Jesus *dies* upon the cross that he saves us. So if saving
and healing are inseparable, it is as Jesus *dies* upon the cross
that he heals us. In the mysterious words of the book of
Isaiah – 'by his wounds we are healed.'

But how can this be? How can the bleeding hand of
Christ restore health to us? How can his dying breath be
our breath of life?

These are deep issues – perhaps too deep for us to fathom
adequately on this side of eternity. I hope that in attempting
an answer I can avoid being glib, or superficial, or hiding
behind religious jargon. Perhaps ordinary human relationships provide the best clues in a search for understanding,

and perhaps the concept of forgiveness provides the best starting point.

It is not hard to see that forgiveness is a basic ingredient in the ministry of Christian healing. Mark 2:1–12 provides a good illustration. A paralysed man was brought to Jesus on a stretcher by four friends. It was no easy task for them because Jesus was in a house packed with people and access to him was blocked by the crowd, but the four friends were determined and resourceful enough to make a hole in the roof and lower the stretcher down in front of Jesus. Their resourcefulness was rewarded. Jesus healed the paralysed man in two stages. The second stage was a simple command to take up his bed and walk, but before that something else had to be said and done, *physical* liberation had to be preceded by *spiritual* liberation, and Jesus sensed that this was so. He sensed that there was a crippling burden of guilt which had to be removed before the body could be released from its paralysis, and so with all the authority which his oneness with the Father gave him he said, 'My son, your sins are forgiven.' And we are told that the paralysed man stood up, picked up his stretcher and went out in the full and astonished view of the whole crowd.

In a similar way sometimes I find that an assurance of forgiveness is an essential pre-requisite of a physical healing. 'Joyce' comes to mind, who came to see me because she suffered from a painful condition of the neck which meant that she had to wear a surgical collar. It eventually emerged that she also suffered from a severe burden of guilt in connection with a sin she had committed many years ago. She told me that every night before she went to sleep she asked the Lord over and over again to forgive her. I was able to share the Christian gospel of forgiveness with her and to suggest a change in her prayers. 'Ask for forgiveness just once more,' I suggested. 'Ask for it simply and trustingly in the name of Jesus, who died on the cross to bring the forgiveness of God to us. Then know that God's forgiveness is yours. You don't have to ask for it any more. Instead of saying "Lord forgive me", say each night, "Thank you, Lord, for forgiving me!"' So Joyce changed her way of thinking and of praying, and not only did her sense of guilt leave her but her neck pains went with it and soon she was able to discard her surgical collar.

In both of these stories the offer of God's forgiveness constituted an explicit element in the ministry of Christian healing. Elsewhere, though it is not explicit, it is certainly implicit — just as I believe it is implicit in every facet of Christian life and ministry.

But what is forgiveness? And how does the death of Jesus bring it to us? Forgiving does not mean forgetting, it means remembering but going on loving just the same. It does not mean ignoring what has been done or putting a false label on an evil act, it means keeping your eyes wide open and yet being prepared to pay the price of maintaining a loving relationship. Even in human terms what a price this can be! I think of 'Grace', a lovely Christian girl, whose husband has for some years been unfaithful to her and is not above treating her with physical violence. She sees precisely what sort of man he is but incredibly she goes on offering him her love. If he were to respond to that love it could make him a new man. Perhaps one day he will come to his senses, but in the meantime Grace goes on loving and forgiving and paying the cost. I believe God treats mankind in a similar way. When God came in Jesus to our confused and fallen world, he came to offer us a relationship with him within which we might recover our senses and our wholeness. Grace can give some slight inkling of the costliness of this offer. It has involved God in loving and forgiving and paying the price of doing so on behalf of the whole human race. And what a price our sins exacted! The price proved to be no less than Christ's own life-blood poured out upon the cross, not just as a tragic miscarriage of justice but as a deliberate sacrificial offering made for the love of you and me.

The cross is a place of pain, but also a place of triumph. Without it there could be no salvation for us. This is why we call the evil day on which human sin did its worst to Jesus *Good* Friday. It was good because on that day Love was true to itself and to us. Love neither compromised nor retreated before the evil and sickness and destructiveness in us. If it had compromised it would have ceased to be Love and would have been irrelevant to our salvation. If it had turned its back and fled it would have ceased to be Love and again would have been irrelevant to us. But Jesus did neither. He stayed the course. He paid the price.

Because of Jesus and the price he has paid I can enter into a saving and healing relationship with God. I can come to God as my real and honest self, not pretending to virtue and wholeness which is not mine, but 'just as I am'. The evil and sickness and destructiveness which is in me will cause him the pain of death, but he takes the pain and death that I cause him and then rises again still offering me the living loving relationship within which I can recover the wholeness for which he made me.

It makes such a difference to know this. I think of 'Greg' whose story was told in detail in chapter 10 of *Christian Healing Rediscovered*. Greg had a hard life and was heavy and sick with the anger he had swallowed back. His suppressed anger gave him all sorts of physical symptoms – headaches, nasal congestion, chest and heart pains, insomnia and with them a black suicidal depression. Underneath it all was smouldering murderous rage against the universe and the God who created it. It was an incredible liberation for Greg when he learned at the cross that God would accept him as he was, that he did not have to hold back and conceal the anger that was consuming him, that the real Greg could meet the real God, could ram on the crown of thorns, smash in the nails, and that the love of God would pay the price, die at his hands and rise again, still offering a relationship within which Greg's own wholeness could be rediscovered and recreated. It was lovely to see Christian healing come to Greg's body, mind and spirit as he encountered Christ on the cross.

Only Love which is prepared to die can enable us to relate to God just as we are, without pretence or self-deception, and only if we come before him as we really are can our healing in depth begin.

There are other factors too which we can discern in the healing power of the suffering and death of Jesus. For instance, some time ago I talked with a man who had been a prisoner-of-war in the second world war. He told me of the help that he had received from the padre in the prisoner-of-

war camp, a padre for whom he had tremendous admiration
because he had turned down an offer of repatriation just in
order to stay with the men he felt called to serve. By contrast I remember being told with some scorn about a certain
clergyman who when he visited a parishioner who was
dangerously ill with an infectious disease stood at the bottom
of the stairs and shouted up, 'Woman, have you made your
peace with God?' The effectiveness of the prisoner-of-war
padre and the ineffectiveness of the parson at the bottom of
the stairs suggest a further line of thought as we seek to
understand the healing power of the cross. It seems that if
we really want to help each other we must be prepared to put
ourselves side by side with those in trouble. The prophet
Ezekiel put it in a nutshell when he wrote, 'I sat where they
sat' (Ezekiel 3:15), and Jesus did just that when in a world
where life is so often painful and bewildering he did not
flinch from sharing and identifying himself with man's pain
and bewilderment.

I think of 'Ellen' who was a mass of insecurity and anxiety.
Her spirit was cringing with feelings of dread and dereliction
which showed themselves in all kinds of strange illogical
fears. If God was to reach her for healing he had to come to
the place where she was. Somehow God had to feel God-
forsaken if he was to share and infiltrate her situation. For
Ellen healing began as she met the crucified Christ who
cried, 'My God, my God, why have you forsaken me!' It is
the healing work of the crucified Christ to be sha. ing the
suffering we endure as well as taking the consequences ol the
suffering we cause.

Of course, Jesus deserved none of it. His death was not
for his deserts. It was for our sins and for our sake and for
our healing. That was how much he loved us. That was how
much he had to love us, if we were to be reconciled with God.
The scriptures say it all. 'In Christ, God reconciled the
world to himself instead of counting men's sins against
them' (2 Corinthians 5:19). 'He personally bore our sins in
his own body on the cross so that we might break with sin
and be alive to all that is good' (1 Peter 2:24). 'He was
wounded for our sins, he was crushed for our wrong doing,
the blows that fell upon him were for our peace, and by his

wounds we are healed' (Isaiah 53:5).

Will you join me in this prayer?

'Lord God, I know that this is a sick world and that my sins are part of the sickness. I also know that, though I do not deserve it, Jesus, your son, has died for my healing. Through the crucified and risen love of Jesus, I am able to come to you, Father, and to find in you forgiveness, and peace, and eternal life. Stir in me the healing power of the Holy Spirit, both for my own wholeness and so that I may myself be a channel of healing in the world, in the name of Jesus. Amen.'

CHAPTER EIGHT

Health Hints from the Bible

The last chapter was an attempt to grapple with some theological questions of considerable depth. By contrast we turn now to some simple practicalities. The Bible is full of health hints based on the principle that 'prevention is better than cure'. This chapter contains just a few of them. If, as a nation, we observed these principles, then without any doubt there would be a dramatic lessening of disease amongst our people. It would seem like a miracle, but the sad fact is that at the moment a great deal of the sickness and disease which preoccupies our National Health Service is self-induced. We could avoid it by paying attention to health hints like the ones which follow. They have been culled from the Bible, but could have been worked out equally on the simple basis of common sense.

(1) It is healthy to cultivate cleanliness in personal habits. The proverb, 'Cleanliness is next to godliness', is not a direct quotation from the Bible, but is well in accord with its spirit, particularly with the elaborate hygiene codes of the Old Testament, which provide detailed instructions for cleanliness in primitive surroundings. All kinds of down-to-earth practicalities of hygiene are covered by the Bible, which even goes as far as specifying the basic requirements for a loo when camping! (See Deuteronomy 23:12–13.)

(2) In the interest of health, care should be taken not to spread infection. Again the hygiene codes of the Old Testament show particular concern about this. For instance Leviticus chapters 13 and 14 contain a variety of anti-infection rules and regulations. Of course, we must not make a fetish of it. There are occasions when we may be required by the love of God to go into places of infection and on these occasions we must trust God's love both for direction and protection.

(3) It is healthy to take physical exercise. Any part of the body can become weak and flabby and even atrophied for the want of it. It is even more important to take mental and spiritual exercise. The first letter to Timothy puts it in this way. 'Bodily exercise is valuable – so far as it goes. But the value of spiritual exercise is without limit.' (1 Timothy 4:8.) Any aptitude of body, mind or spirit is like the talents in the parable of Jesus. Anything we do not use, we lose.

(4) If exercise is important, so too is rest. Genesis 2 tells us that God 'rested' on the sabbath day, and it is the fourth commandment that men too should observe a day of rest (Exodus 20:8–11). This is a law of health and efficiency. I remember breaking it as a student at Oxford when the pressure of work was becoming particularly hard and then finding that not only was I less fit but surprisingly I covered less ground working seven days out of seven than I could cover by working for six days and then having Sunday off work.

(5) Healthy living involves keeping a watch on what we eat and drink. St. Paul warns against the attitude of those 'whose god is their belly'. (Philippians 3:19.) The book of Proverbs warns that 'the drunkard and the glutton come to poverty' (Proverbs 23:21), and the same chapter contains a colourful description of the miseries the heavy drinker brings on himself. 'Who's got trouble? Who's got misery? Who gets bad tempered and quarrelsome? Who gets bruises without knowing why? Who gets bloodshot eyes? The pub-crawler who spends hours swilling one drink after another! Don't let the sparkle and smooth taste of strong drink deceive you. In the end it bites like a snake and is as venomous as a cobra. Your eyes will play you tricks. Your speech will be confused. You will feel like a man tossing out at sea, swaying about at the top of a ship's mast. You will feel like someone who has been beaten up without even knowing it was happening. And next day you'll go on drinking and it will all happen again!' (Proverbs 23:29–35.) Of course, Jesus was not himself tee-total. He enjoyed a good meal, a good party, a drink with his friends (e.g. Luke 5:29–34). If we follow him our enjoyment of our food and drink will be enhanced by his blessing and his presence. But that same presence will help us not to use our food and drink in a damaging or destructive

way, St. Paul puts the principle simply and positively –
'Whether you eat or drink, or whatever you do, do it all to
the glory of God.' (1 Corinthians 10:31.)

(6) This text provides a test question for other forms of
intake also. Can one imagine a drug addict injecting heroin
into the veins of a pock-marked abscessed arm – to the glory
of God? Can one imagine a chain-smoker pumping nicotine
into his lungs – to the glory of God? Of course not. Mind
you, it is certainly not the case that we believe in a 'kill-joy'
God. Joy is God's nature and God's business. Nor is it the
case that God is only interested in what is good for the soul,
and not in the body. God the Father made my body. God the
Son shared a similar body. God the Holy Spirit wants my
body as his home. It is precisely because God values my body
that I cannot mishandle or poison it with his blessing or to
his glory.

(7) Since body, mind and spirit are interrelated, my health
depends not only on how I feed my body but also on how I
feed my mind and spirit. Mental and spiritual poisoning are
even more dangerous than physical poisoning. Positive thinking is a basic ingredient of health. In St. Paul's famous words
– 'Whatever things are true, whatever things are honourable,
whatever things are just, whatever things are pure, whatever
things are lovely, whatever things are of good repute, whatever strikes you as excellent, whatever strikes you as admir-
able – these are the things with which to fill your minds.'
(Philippians 4:8.) This is the essence of the nature of worship
– fixing our attention upon and filling our souls with the
highest and best that we know, God's own revealed nature.

(8) We have ranged fairly briskly over the biblical health
hints itemized so far, but I want to deal with the final item
on my list in rather greater detail. It is the teaching of the
Christian faith that a wholesome sexual morality is a basic
and necessary ingredient in a healthy society and that we
reject it at our peril both as individuals and as a nation. The
pungent instruction of St. Paul is – 'Avoid sexual looseness
like the plague!' (1 Corinthians 6:18). Avoid practising it.
Avoid talking about it. Avoid slavering over it. 'Live your
lives in love – the same sort of love which Christ gives us. But
as for sexual immorality in all its forms, don't even talk about

such things! Of this much you can be quite certain. Neither the immoral nor the dirty-minded man has any inheritance in Christ's kingdom. Don't let anyone fool you on this point, however plausible his argument.' (From Ephesians 5:1–6.)

As I write these words I am well aware that morality is under attack in our nation at present and that 'permissive' views are widespread. They have infiltrated the media to an alarming degree. For instance, recently I listened to a publisher of pornographic magazines arguing on BBC Radio 4 that there is no reason why 'good quality pornography' should not be left around lying on the coffee table in any truly 'liberated' household. In favour of that programme it could at least be said that the plea for pornography was an open and explicit presentation of a case. Listeners could identify the speaker and his philosophy and form their own opinions about the value of and motives behind what he was saying. But all too often the procedure is more insidious and the listener or viewer finds himself absorbing amoral or immoral attitudes, almost without knowing that it is happening. Some comedy shows are the worst offenders – including many programmes which are regarded as family entertainment. A typical example was provided in a comedy show screened early one evening on Granada TV. One of the characters could not think of a word to describe a male virgin and asked, 'What do you call a fellow who doesn't have sex before he marries?' The answer came like a shot – 'Boring!' There was a giggle from the studio audience. But in fact is it really funny to titter or slaver over promiscuity? And is it as harmless as the media seem to think it is? Is Christian sexual morality really as dull and outmoded as the pedlars of permissiveness suggest? Or are there sound and compelling reasons for upholding it?

I had to find answers to questions like these at a very early stage in my life as a clergyman. I remember 'Polly', a pretty vivacious teenage brunette who belonged to the youth club I ran as a curate. She came to my study one day and wanted to know whether I could make any sort of reasonable case for chastity. She said she had been on holiday abroad. She had met a handsome young Spaniard. They had had intercourse one evening on the beach. 'I enjoyed it,' she said, 'and

I am going to go on having sex when I fancy it, unless you can give me really good reasons why I shouldn't.'

I remember groping around for an answer, knowing that none of the time-honoured moralizing clichés would do any good. Whether 'Polly' was convinced by what I said I am not sure, but subsequently the more I thought about it the more it seemed to me that there are very strong reasons indeed for the Christian conviction that chastity is right and wholesome and that promiscuity is wrong and sick.

St. Paul gives the clue when, before condemning promiscuity, he first affirms the importance of love. 'Live your lives in love – but as for sexual immorality, don't even talk about it!' Love is the supreme ingredient in full and healthy living. Life is for loving. People are for loving. Sex is for loving.

The basic factor about promiscuity which makes it wrong and unwholesome is that it is fundamentally and demonstrably *unloving*. In the first place, *it is not loving* to spread disease. There is no doubt that promiscuity does so. We are at the moment in the middle of a national venereal disease epidemic. There is an odd conspiracy of silence about it. Christians find it distasteful to talk about it. The merchants of permissiveness find it politic to ignore it. But the horrific truth is that gonorrhoea is our second most common infectious disease after measles! There are a thousand or more new cases of it every week, and they are becoming increasingly resistant to treatment. But gonorrhoea, syphilis, non-gonococcal urethritis and other forms of V.D. all have this in common. They are completely unnecessary because if promiscuity were to end the V.D. epidemic would also end. Secondly *it is not loving* to bring unwanted children into the world. Contrary to popular superstition, contraceptives are not fool-proof and human beings are certainly not fool-proof in the use of them. The result is hundreds of thousands of unwanted pregnancies. Thirdly *it is not loving* to treat people as less than people, to use people as things. This is what casual sex does. It regards another human being as a sexual stimulant rather than as a person.

Of course the cry goes up in certain circles that we do ourselves emotional damage if we do not have experience of premarital intercourse. In fact, the truth is precisely the opposite – or so it seems from people I have dealt with. I can think of 'Colin', scared to death because he thought he had V.D., or 'Judy', afraid she was pregnant and completely in a panic when her fear made her miss a couple of periods, or 'John and Sally' who regularly had intercourse before they were married but found that after marriage they were incapable of intercourse. They had preconditioned themselves to all the wrong surroundings and stimuli. They are divorced now. Promiscuity leaves a trail of emotional damage in its wake because it is not healthy or responsible or personal.

'Polly' was hooked on the notion that promiscuity means enjoyment, that permissiveness is the royal road to the good life. But as one of our local doctors said to me a few days before I wrote this chapter, all the evidence seems to point precisely the opposite way. When you leave out the self-discipline of real love, what is left is a poor thing, however many kicks you may get out of it for a start.

Later I was to meet 'Rod and Barbara'. They were different. They said, 'We're engaged. We're in love. One day we shall be married. It can't possibly be wrong for us.' But again, judged purely from the standpoint of their own satisfaction and fulfilment, are they right? The great thing about an engagement is that it is *not* the same as marriage. It can be broken. Sometimes it should be broken. It is part of the concept of engagement that one can 'disengage' without spoiling another life or lessening the freshness and uniqueness of one's own marriage when it happens.

A great deal depends on one's first experience of intercourse. It is important that there should be relaxation, security, lack of inhibition and above all *meaningfulness*. The amount of joy we receive from sexual intercourse depends on the *meaning* it has for us. When it means complete self-giving, complete sharing, complete loving, complete commitment, it is a tremendous thing. Where commitment is incomplete, as it is in an engagement, intercourse has less meaning and is a lesser thing. Where commitment is nil, as in promiscuous sex, the sex act means little or nothing, and to throw away one's first experience of intercourse and precondition subsequent experiences of intercourse in this way is one of the saddest forms of waste.

Listen to Mark's record of the way in which Jesus talked to the people of his own day. He might just as well have been talking to us. 'You know so little of the meaning of love,' he said. He quoted Genesis 2:24 to the effect that 'a man shall leave his father and mother and shall join in one flesh with his wife,' and he commented, 'They are no longer two people, but one,' (Mark 10:6–8). That is Christ's great concept of the closest of all relationships, the man-woman entity, the 'joining together in one flesh'. This, he says, is the purpose of our sexuality – and nothing less.

Perhaps I may end this chapter with a little personal testimony to this 'one flesh' relationship of which Jesus speaks. I believe that a loving Christian marriage is one of the greatest and most precious things in the world. It is well worth preparing for. It is well worth waiting for. I can never be sufficiently grateful to the Christian faith for leading me to it. Next to the love of the Lord, the love of my wife is the best thing in my life. To exchange it for the poisoned perks of promiscuous living would not only be disobedience to Christ – it would also be the poorest deal I could possibly imagine!

CHAPTER NINE

The Ministry of Deliverance

We have already thought about the Christian church's curious blind spot, which has for centuries led to a neglect of the ministry of healing. 'Preach and heal' was Christ's dual commission to the church. As far as preaching is concerned the church has certainly made an effort to be obedient to the command. Over the centuries millions of sermons of one sort or another have been delivered at millions of services Sunday after Sunday. But the second part of the commission 'Preach *and heal*' has dropped out of sight during much of the history of the church, though in our time it seems belatedly to be coming back into view.

I want now to suggest that there is a further blind spot in the life of today's church. People whose eyes have been opened to the importance of the ministry of healing can still be unaware of the importance of what is sometimes called 'exorcism' and sometimes, more helpfully, 'the ministry of deliverance'.

This was pointed out to me by a retired naval captain and his wife, Jimmy and Fynvola James, who wrote to me in 1975 from their home in Northwood, Middlesex, after they had read a series of articles of mine in the Church of England Newspaper about Christian healing. They drew my attention to the fact that before Jesus sent out the Twelve on the healing and teaching mission recorded in Luke 9:1–6, he specifically authorized and empowered them to cast out demons (verse 1). Similarly, after the healing and teaching mission conducted by seventy disciples (Luke 10: 1–20), they returned full of joy saying, 'Lord, even demons are subject to us in your name,' (verse 17). There are twenty-eight recorded instances of the ministry of deliverance in the gospels (as compared with fifty-two reports of healings and forty-

seven instances of preaching the gospel) and a further ten
instances of the ministry of deliverance in Acts (as compared with eleven reports of healing and thirty-six instances
of preaching the gospel). In the accounts of deliverance
(like those of healing) some instances concern a single person, but some are multiple events involving a ministry to
many people. 'In my name,' said Jesus, 'believers will cast
out demons,' (Mark 16:17). And so they did.

And so do Captain and Mrs James. Since 1972 they have
felt called to minister deliverance to over two hundred individuals whose lives have been burdened in some way,
especially by fear or impurity or by occult influences. In
1977 they were kind enough to invite me to stay with them,
and they spent some hours sharing their convictions about
this ministry with me.

I suppose that I reacted with a mixture of feelings – as
so many people in today's church do. It seems such a weird
form of ministry, and indeed in some cases it is so. For
instance, a colleague tells me that when during the course
of an exorcism he touched a parishioner who had become
involved in occult practices, he was literally thrown across
the room by a force like electricity. Captain and Mrs James
tell me that their ministry of deliverance is sometimes
attended by shouting, screaming, and coughing up quantities
of mucus, and they keep a 'deliverance kit' of a plastic bowl
and paper tissues at hand to 'catch the demons'! It all sounds
very odd.

There is a further difficulty too. Many Christians are
not at all sure whether they believe in the devil and his hoard
of demons. There seem to be three opinions within the
Christian church. First there are those who believe in the
devil and his demons quite literally. Secondly there are those
who regard this sort of language as a symbolic and per-
sonalized way of speaking of the evil which is to be found
in the heart of man, for which we have nobody to blame but
ourselves. Thirdly there are those who are prepared to take
the devil literally but not demons. Of the three the third
view is, I think, the least logical. To attribute all temptation
to the direct activity of a single unaided devil is to credit him
with an omnipresence which can properly be attributed only

to God. If he exists as an actual being, created by God but having fallen away and now exercising himself in malevolent opposition to God's purpose as the tempter and would-be destroyer of the human race, then the common occurrence of temptation and evil suggests that since he is not and cannot be omnipresent he has other fallen spirits working under him like a sort of Mafia.

With regard to the choice between a literal or a symbolic interpretation of the devil and his demons, every Christian must weigh the evidence and come to his or her own decision. Although many have a revulsion against the literal view, there are three things at least which can be urged in its favour. It does seem that Jesus believed in the devil and in demons literally. Also, the fact that the devil and demons are normally beyond the awareness of our senses is not a conclusive reason for rejecting them. Science has shown us there are colours we cannot see with the human eye, sounds we cannot hear with the human ear, concepts we cannot encompass with the human mind. It is a mysterious universe in which we live. We know only a small fraction of it. Furthermore, there is an increasing amount of attested evidence which strongly suggests the existence of the demonic. Some of it comes from the mission field, some from psychological studies or psychical research, and some from the more baffling areas of ordinary pastoral experience.

Perhaps the important thing to grasp is that though there may be doubt as to whether a man can be possessed or oppressed by a personal 'evil spirit', there can be no doubt whatsoever that life can be disturbed and distorted by all sorts of aspects of evil. Any of us can be troubled by a spirit of fear or lust or greed or hate. Whether or not that spirit is a demonic, personal being, or a diseased element of our own personality, or indeed both, in any event it is important to realize that such a spirit is completely alien to God's purpose and perfection and that our Lord Jesus Christ has both the will and the power to cast it out. There are two paramount truths which the Christian church must never forget. There is the negative truth of the fact of evil, the deadliness of evil, its insidious power to deceive and to tempt, and there is the positive truth that when Christ confronts any element of evil in us his invariable and uncompromising will is to cast it out. When he does so sin *must* begin to break its hold upon us *unless* we interpose our own free will as a barrier against him, cuddling and protecting the evil in us against Christ's mighty delivering power.

There are perhaps three main implications of this in the life of an ordinary church.

First, if we have to have an encounter with any sort of occult force, we can do so with the quiet assurance that the power of God in Jesus Christ is stronger than the power of evil. Generally speaking I do not believe that most of us are called to seek out encounters with the dark world of the occult, but if it happens to come our way we can meet it without fear in the name of Jesus Christ. There is an instance of this sort of encounter at the end of chapter fourteen of *Christian Healing Rediscovered*. Two teenage girls 'Franchette' and 'Josephine' had become mixed up in a circle which dabbled in the occult and Franchette had become a very troubled person in consequence, dogged by a sense of an evil presence, as though something malevolent was continually walking behind her. Even though the girls had withdrawn from practices connected with the occult the sense of the evil presence persisted. Through the Christian ministry of deliverance I was able to liberate Franchette from this. Was it some sort of demon afflicting her or was it all in her mind? Perhaps there is no way of knowing. What is beyond dispute is that she was a deeply disturbed girl. It is also clear that the power of Christ proved stronger than whatever was harming her.

Sometimes we may be called to exercise this ministry upon a place rather than a person. Recently I was asked to do this in a house where some sort of alien presence had been felt. Again the authoritative affirmation of the presence and power of Christ seemed all that was needed, and at the time of writing there has been no recurrence of the trouble.

A second occasion for the ministry of deliverance may be provided by ordinary mental or physical conditions where there is no hint of an occult factor, but where nonetheless one has an intuition that not only is there a hurt to be soothed and healed, but there is something evil or alien to

God's purpose that needs to be driven out. I think of 'Craig', who had a strange depression. There seemed no physical reason for it and it did not respond to an ordinary laying on of hands. Also it did not seem to fit into any of the ordinary patterns of neurosis which I have been taught to look for when dealing with a depression. Hours of counselling left the condition completely untouched. Then on an impulse one day, instead of addressing Craig himself I spoke directly to whatever it was that was hurting him. I told 'it', whatever 'it' was, that it was alien to God's purpose, that it was damaging one whom the Father loves, one for whom Christ died, and firmly, quietly, unemotionally, in the name of Jesus Christ I rebuked it and commanded it to go. There has been no further trouble. Craig has been well to this day.

I have just been writing to a friend who is suffering from cancer and have felt moved to write about both Christian healing and Christian deliverance. I am sure she will not object if I quote part of the letter:

Do continue to practise the presence of Christ. Remember his words, 'I am with you always.' Picture him. As you look at him he looks at you. As he looks at you, his gaze is charged with love and power and healing. He also sees the cancer which is burdening you, and as he looks at 'it' as distinct from 'you' his gaze changes. Can you picture his eyes as he pictures the cancer itself? Can you see the rebuke in his eyes for it, because it is spoiling and hurting someone who is infinitely precious to the Father? This rebuke, combined with the might of Godhead together, makes his gaze rather like a laser beam cutting into and diminishing and destroying the cancer's power. Picture him. Relax into God's strength. Say quietly and confidently, 'Thy will be done,' which means, 'Thy holy and and healing will be done, to the casting out of all that hurts and to the establishment of God's perfection in me, in my body, my mind, my spirit.' Say it quietly, firmly, trustingly.

It seems increasingly right to me to bring this dual approach of healing and deliverance to many conditions.

5

The third sphere to which the ministry of deliverance is relevant is one which is so obvious that it is odd that we so often neglect it. We believe in a Christ who accepts us just as we are. 'Accept one another,' says St. Paul, 'as Christ accepted you.' (Romans 15:7.) But an accepting Christ is not the same as a permissive Christ. Though Jesus loves and accepts me in depth, though I can come to him 'just as I am', this does not mean that his purpose for me is that I should be less than my truest and best self; it does not mean that he connives and winks at my sins. It is precisely because Jesus loves me in depth that he is hostile to all that diminishes or falsifies me. If there is a spirit of fear or lust or greed or hate in me, if any sin or any negativity of body, mind or spirit is hurting or spoiling me, Jesus will inevitably and inexorably set about the process of casting it out. Exposure to this ministry of deliverance is part and parcel of being a Christian.

I think of 'Beatrice' who had a spirit of hate for her step-mother. It was in a sense justifiable because her step-mother had ill-treated her, but it hurt and diminished her. She knew that it was the will of Jesus to cast out this hatred. She knew she had to choose between the spirit of hatred and Jesus, and though it was not easy she made the right choice. I think of 'Ralph' who had begun to be a Christian but looked so miserable. The fact was, he was being unfaithful to his wife and he knew that he had to choose between Jesus and his adultery. Finally he made the right choice, and even before he told me I knew he had done so, because he looked so much happier.

As Jesus stands before you and me here and now, he looks into us, sees us exactly as we are, loves us with the deepest, most powerful love we will ever know, identifies those elements in us which are alien to the will of God and alien to our own true selves and he says to those elements, 'Come out of him,' or 'Come out of her.' He says it without compromise or equivocation. He says it with God's own authority.

Perhaps we have a clue here to one of the reasons why some people stay away from church, though it is hardly ever admitted as such. Folk give a variety of reasons for staying away from worship. They say, 'The church is too draughty.' The pews are too hard. Or perhaps the church is so modern that it doesn't look like a church at all. The churchmanship is too high. Or too low. The Vicar's no good. The organist is no good. The choir is no good. The services are old fashioned. Or they've gone all new-fangled and we're not having that! The congregation are religious prigs. Or they're a lot of hypocrites and haven't an ounce of true religion in them. There's too much emotion. Or there isn't enough. And it is all a bit out of date in modern Britain, isn't it? And in any case, we're all very busy these days aren't we?

People say all these things and some of them are probably true. But at a deeper level, though nobody admits it, is it not true that people stay away because they are afraid that per-haps – just perhaps – they may be confronted with the fact of sin and with the fact that it is the work of Christ and his church to expose and exorcize that sin? Deep down do not many of us experience an urge to stay away from Christ simply because we are plain scared of what he may cast out from us? In biblical times candidates for exorcism pleaded with Jesus to go away. Times have not changed and neither has human nature.

Spiritual surgery is as unattractive to us as surgery upon our body – perhaps more so. However, we need not be afraid. Jesus only casts out things that are worthless or harm-ful, and he *never* leaves a vacuum, because any emptiness left after Christ's ministry of deliverance can be more than filled by the resources of the Holy Spirit.

So, to summarize, the work of Jesus is not just to soothe and heal the hurts of our bodies, minds and spirits. It is also to cast out that which causes the hurt. We may identify what hurts either as a demon which has an existence independent of ourselves, or as a sinful or harmful habit, attitude or element which we have acquired for ourselves or had foisted upon us by a fallen world. There is probably no harm in this division of opinion as long as we recognize that either way it is the work of Christ's church to meet this situation as Jesus himself would have done. So, Father, 'Deliver us from evil,' and make us channels of Christian deliverance in this oppressed world.

CHAPTER TEN

'Thy Will Be Done'

It is arguable that the words 'Thy will be done' are the most misunderstood part of the Lord's Prayer. In fact perhaps they constitute one of the most misunderstood phrases in the whole of the New Testament. We tend to think of them as a sort of sigh of resignation. They are sometimes used, for instance, if we are ill and our illness does not respond either to medical treatment or to prayers for healing. If the expectation of recovery fades and we face the prospect of suffering and perhaps death, we may find ourselves praying, 'Thy will be done.' If we mean by this that God can be trusted no matter how difficult and perplexing life may be, then we could do and say nothing better. But if we are somehow implying that we must resign ourselves to the disease, the suffering and the death because God has planned just this for us, then we misunderstand the nature of prayer and the nature of God to a tragic and almost blasphemous degree!

God's will is always consistent with his goodness, his strength and his love. It is a will for our wholeness in body, mind and spirit. The fact that we are all less than whole in body, mind and spirit may be due in any given case to a variety of factors. We may individually bring it on ourselves. We may be suffering from the sins and folly of society. We may be the victims of heredity. Circumstance, environment and accident may all play their part. But the one thing of which we can be absolutely certain is that it cannot be attributed to the will of God. Think for instance of the many occasions on which lepers approached Jesus for healing. Did he ever say anything like this? 'Oh no, my lad, I have no intention of healing you. Your leprous skin is what God wills for you. The claw-hand and stumpy foot which the leprosy is producing is all part of God's design. You are going blind in one eye because that is God's intention. You must bear it all submissively and say, "God's will be done." ' Of course not! He knew that his Father's will was for wholeness, and in the name of that will he rebuked all that afflicted or marred the body, mind and spirit of man.

In other words, 'Thy will be done' is not a sigh of resignation. It is more like a battle-cry. May God's holy, healing and mighty will prevail – rebuking all that is alien to the perfection of his creative purpose – cleansing, purging, recreating, making whole!

Anyone who accepts this is well on the way to that attitude of mind which makes healing seem a natural, logical and even inevitable element in all Christian life and ministry. However, there are some thoughtful Bible-oriented Christians who have a problem here. If this is not your problem you may wonder what all the fuss is about in the next few pages. So do feel free to miss out the rest of this chapter. The general argument of the book will not suffer. But if this is your problem, it could be the single factor which keeps you from the ministry of healing, and it is important that it should be taken seriously.

The difficulty which troubles some people is that although there is in the Bible a tremendous emphasis on healing, and although one of the titles given to God is 'the LORD who heals' (Exodus 15:26), there are also passages, particularly in the Old Testament, which suggest that God also causes disease and death.

It is perhaps not too hard to understand why disease and death may come upon those who oppose God and resist his will, as in the story of the plagues (Exodus 7–12), or the case of Ananias and Sapphira (Acts 5:1–11), because if turning towards God means turning towards life and health, then logically turning away from God will involve a movement away from life and health. But what are we to make of instances where it is God's own faithful servants who suffer in this way?

Perhaps the best way to seek light on this issue is to undertake a study of an actual Bible passage which embodies the problem. So here in Today's English Version is most of Exodus 4:19–26. I can think of no Bible passage which bristles with greater difficulties from the viewpoint of Christian healing.

> While Moses was still in Midian, the LORD said to him, 'Go back to Egypt . . . ' So Moses took his wife and his sons, put them on a donkey, and set out with them for Egypt . . . Again the LORD said to Moses, 'Now that you are going back to Egypt, be sure to perform before the king all the miracles which I have given you the power to do. But I will make the king stubborn, and he will not let the people go . . . ' At a camping place on the way to Egypt, the LORD met Moses and tried to kill him. Then Zipporah, his wife, took a sharp stone, cut off the foreskin of her son, and touched Moses' genitals with it. Because of the rite of circumcision she said to Moses, 'You are a husband of blood to me.' And so the LORD spared Moses' life.

A thoroughly horrid story! There are various unpleasant elements in it. Let us see if we can isolate and understand them as we reconstruct the scene.

God, we are told, tried to kill Moses, although he was about the Lord's business at the time, because he had been ordered to go to Egypt and was on his way in obedience to the order. I take it that the meaning of this odd statement is that on the way to Egypt Moses became critically ill.

The fact that Moses became so ill while in the service of 'the LORD who heals' would itself present something of a problem, but the problem is intensified a hundredfold when we are told incredibly that the illness was the Lord's doing. Whatever are we to make of the bald words of the text – 'The LORD met Moses and tried to kill him?'

There are various factors which we have to take into account here. It is sometimes said that though the Bible is God's revelation it is a progressive revelation. God shows only a little of himself at a time. Thus the level of revelation in, say, the Book of Judges is appreciably lower than that in John's gospel. According to this theory we are at a fairly primitive level of revelation in the story from Exodus 4 and we must interpret it bearing that in mind.

Perhaps, however, this is not quite the right way of describing the process of revelation. It seems not altogether accurate to speak of 'God's progressive revelation'. I believe it is always God's will to share the truth about himself with us completely. Anything less would not be consonant with his goodness and his love. However, though I do not believe in God's progressive revelation I do believe in man's progressive perception of God's self-revelation. This is the way it has been in my own life. I can see more of God's nature now than I could ten years ago. Hopefully in another ten years I may see more still. God does not change, but my receptiveness does. Similarly in the history of man, although God is consistent our level of receptiveness is not.

Generation by generation man has become open to new truths. This does not mean that the graph of man's spiritual awareness has climbed upwards steadily or evenly. There have been peaks and troughs. But each new generation has had the opportunity to benefit from the spiritual insights of past generations, and so, by and large, a forward movement can be discerned in the history of Israel as recorded in the Bible. One of the great insights that can be found in the book of Exodus is that whereas the Egyptians worshipped a plurality of widely differing deities the God of Israel is One. 'I am the LORD thy God. Thou shalt have no other gods . . . ' (Exodus 20:1-3, AV). It follows therefore in Exodus that all that happens, even the illness of Moses, must be related to the One God. Subsequently other insights were accepted. Isaiah saw the holiness of God very clearly. Hosea saw new dimensions of the love of God. It followed that the unholy and the unloving could not arise directly from the will of God. But for this insight the Israelites had to wait till they were ready, and the full and supreme perception of God's nature was to come later still – to and through Jesus. Knowing this, it is important that we should look at the Old Testament through the lens of the New Testament, and that we should look at the New Testament through the lens of Jesus himself.

There is another factor which has to be considered in weighing the story of Moses' illness. It is a point of Hebrew idiom and is vital for understanding both this story and many

others in the Bible. In English idiom we distinguish clearly
between consequence and purpose. If I happen to bang my
head against a wall and so I get a bruise, that is consequence.
If because of some strange masochistic impulse I bang my
head against a wall in order to get a bruise, that is purpose.
We distinguish clearly between the two, but Hebrew idiom
makes no such distinction. Consequence and purpose are
blurred together and both are expressed in a 'purpose-type'
manner. Thus if God sent Moses to Egypt and in consequence he became ill, in Hebrew idiom 'God made him ill'.
Similarly, if God tells Moses to speak his word to Pharaoh
but as a consequence Pharaoh hardens his heart, in Hebrew
idiom 'God has hardened Pharaoh's heart'. Later Isaiah is
sent to proclaim God's word to the Israelites, but the consequence is that they stop their ears and shut their eyes and
harden their hearts. In Hebrew idiom the instruction which
God gives to Isaiah is, 'Make the heart of this people fat,
and their ears heavy, and shut their eyes, lest they see with
their eyes and hear with their ears and understand with their
heart and turn again and be healed.' (Isaiah 6:10.)

Even the Greek of the New Testament sometimes be-
haves in a Hebrew manner and follows Hebrew idiom. When
Jesus is telling the disciples that though they themselves will
see the point of his parables many others will hear the stories
but completely fail to discern their meaning, he follows
Hebrew idiom and says, 'Unto you is given the mystery of
the kingdom of God: but unto them that are without, all
things are done in parables: that seeing they may see, and not
perceive; and hearing they may hear, and not understand;
lest haply they should turn again, and it should be forgiven
them.' (Mark 4:11–12.) That is the translation offered by
the 1881 revision of the Authorized Version, which is highly
literal in its approach. The Living Bible correctly takes the
purposive element out of these verses and translates, 'You are
permitted to know some truths about the Kingdom of God
that are hidden to those outside the Kingdom: "Though they
see and hear, they will not understand or turn to God, or
be forgiven for their sins." ' However, unfortunately I know
of no modern translation which does this consistently in
every instance. So the biblical interpreter must always be on

the watch for the occurrence of this idiom and take care
not to give it the force of absolute theological truth. The
idiom crops up in all kinds of unexpected places. It even
comes in the Lord's Prayer. 'Lead us not into temptation'
does not mean that God tempts us. It means that he has put
us into a world where temptation is a consequence of life
and we therefore need to pray for his protection. It is left to
St. James to break the idiom and to say plainly, 'Let no one
say when he is tempted, "I am tempted by God"; for God
cannot be tempted with evil and he himself tempts no one;'
(James 1:13). So in our thinking about the Lord's Prayer
we should re-introduce the distinction between consequence
and purpose which the Hebrew, and to some extent the
Greek idiom has blurred, and translate: 'Save us from giving
way to temptation,' or 'Do not let us be tested past our
breaking-point.'

Therefore, if we are to employ an English rather than a
Hebrew idiom, God does not tempt us. Equally in English
idiom God did not try to kill Moses. Why then in God's
world did Moses become critically ill while about God's
business? Not because this was God's will. God made us in
his own image (Genesis 1:26–27). It is his will that our
bodies, our minds and our spirits should reflect his own
wholeness. 'Be perfect,' or 'Be complete,' said Jesus, 'just like
your heavenly Father.' (Matthew 5:48.) Nothing less is
God's will. However, part of the mystery of the universe is
that God, though he is almighty, allows human freedom to
have its way, even when that way is sinful and foolish, because if he were to destroy our freedom he would destroy us
in doing so. Thus God's will is for our peace, but century
after century we make war. God's will is for our wholeness,
but century after century we bring sickness upon ourselves
and upon each other, upon society as a whole and upon
generations to come. Yet through it all God remains 'the
LORD who heals'. If we make ourselves available to his influence we are making ourselves available to healing.

Moses was in fact healed. But the story does not run out
of problems at this point, because the method of his healing
was odd in the extreme. Zipporah, his wife, was a Midianite,
and she seems to have made a primitive Midianite blood

offering to extend the life of her husband. Did it help?
Probably not, except that before she made it she believed
that Moses was dying, whereas afterwards she believed he
would get better. There is no doubt that when we are ill,
the attitude of those around us is a major factor in our
recovery or our failure to recover. The replacement of a
negative attitude with a positive one on Zipporah's part
could do nothing but good and, in fact, the illness receded
afterwards.

There is an interesting sequel to this story. Though Zipporah felt she had saved her husband's life, she also seemed
to feel angry at doing so at the expense of her son. As soon
as the threat to Moses' life receded, Zipporah and her sons
went back to Midian and Moses went on weak and alone.
The odd thing was that though when Moses was fit and
powerful and certain of himself none of his fellow country-
men listened to him (Exodus 2:13–14), now in his mental
turmoil and bodily weakness God is seen to speak and act
through him. First Aaron followed his lead, and then the
Israelites as a whole did so. 'They believed, and when they
heard that the Lord had come to them . . . they bowed
down and worshipped' (Exodus 4:31). When Moses was at
his weakest, paradoxically then he was strong for God. God
had not caused his illness, but he used it to make Moses more
transparent for his own purposes. 'All things work together
for good for those who love God,' (Romans 8:28). The
apostle Paul had a similar experience. He suffered from
what he termed 'a thorn in the flesh, a messenger of Satan to
harass me' (2 Corinthians 12:7). He prayed for its removal,
but for some reason the trouble remained. However, within
the trouble came this assurance from God – 'My grace is
sufficient for you, for my strength is made perfect in weakness' (2 Corinthians 12:9). We are uncertain what the
trouble was. George Bennett, who died shortly before this
book was completed but who taught me so much about
Christian healing in the closing years of his life, thought
it may have been shingles of the head. All kinds of other
suggestions have been made, including epilepsy, ophthalmia
and malarial fever. Whatever it was, it did not come from
God and was not God's will. It came from Satan. Paul says

so. But God outmanoeuvred Satan and turned his own 'messenger' against him.

To summarize this chapter, God's will is for wholeness, for health of body, mind and spirit. 'Bless the LORD, O my soul,' says the psalmist, 'and forget not all his benefits; who forgives all your iniquity and heals all your diseases,' (Psalm 103:2–3). Jesus came into the world to do the will of God (John 6:38), and so it follows inevitably that the will of Christ for us is again for wholeness. One of the few occasions on which Jesus is said to have been angry was when his will to heal was doubted. ' "If only you will," ' said a leper, ' "you can cleanse me." In warm indignation Jesus . . . said: "Indeed I will." ' (Mark 1:40–41, as translated in the New English Bible.) If God's will to heal is somehow frustrated, he will find other ways of bringing good from the situation. But he remains 'the LORD who heals' and his primary will remains that of the restoration of our perfect wholeness. And it is that will for healing and deliverance which is activated and reinforced when in Christ's own words we pray to the God whom he has revealed to us – 'Thy will be done.'

CHAPTER ELEVEN

Another Glimpse of Jesus

Some people tell me that the part of my earlier book which they found most helpful is the chapter called 'A Glimpse of Jesus', in which we looked at Luke 5:12–32 in order to see the healing ministry of Jesus actually in progress. We saw Jesus making a leper clean, healing a paralysed man, and then calling Levi, better known as Matthew, from his work collecting taxes for the Romans to full-time Christian service, and I suggested that all three events were instances of Christian healing of body, mind or spirit.

The passage was almost taken at random, because virtually any passage from any of the gospels proves on examination to be rich in instances of or insights about Christian healing. This present book would not be complete unless again we spend some time, in the words of the Letter to the Hebrews, with 'our eyes fixed on Jesus, on whom faith depends from start to finish' (Hebrews 12:2 NEB). So at this point we shall allow ourselves the privilege of once again looking at and listening to our healing Lord, with the help of Luke. We take up his story at the point at which we left it before, chapter 5, verse 33, and will stay with it till chapter 6, verse 19.

After his conversion Levi had a big party. He had met Jesus. He was happy. He wanted his friends and neighbours to meet Jesus and be happy too. But this seemed all wrong to some people. They said, 'The disciples of John the Baptist live a life of fasting and praying, and it is the same with the Pharisees. So why are yours eating and drinking?' They thought that religious people should look severe, sombre and strait-laced at all times. They remind me of a girl in my Sunday School class who implored me just before my ordination – 'Don't do it, Mr Lawrence. Just think,

you won't never be able to smoke, you won't never be able
to drink, you won't never be able to have any fun any more.'
A fine Sunday School teacher I had been! I had certainly
failed to communicate the joy and positivity of the gospel
to her.

Of course there are occasions when Christians are called
to be sad. Because we are sinners we must be sorry for our
sins so that we may be receptive to our Father's forgiveness.
Also, if we have any love in us, we shall sometimes find ourselves called to share the world's suffering and sadness in
some way. And occasionally we may find ourselves in the
doldrums because we are resisting God's will in some way
and the inner tussle produces a sort of therapeutic misery-
patch until we have the sense to see that God's way is best.
But having said all that, it still remains true that at the
heart of Christian life and experience there is joy – the joy of
knowing Jesus, and through him the joy of knowing that his
Father is our Father, and his universe is our home. All
material things are fashioned by our Father's hand – the food
we eat and the beauties of nature we enjoy. Our enjoyment
of the world is part of our union with Christ.

As Jesus put it, 'Do wedding guests fast while celebrating
with the groom? Of course not,' though he added a dark
hint of his coming crucifixion: 'The time will come when the
bridegroom will be taken from them. That will be the time
to fast.'

Then Jesus turned the conversation to a more important
matter than fasting, using as so often the parable method to
make his point. He said – 'No one tears a piece off a new
coat to patch up an old one. If he did, the new coat would
have a hole in it and the old one would have a piece that
didn't match. And no one puts new wine into old wine-
skins. The new wine would burst the skins. You would spoil
the skins and spill the wine.'

The point is that Christianity is not just the old Jewish
religion with one or two new ideas added. It is something
completely new. When a man becomes a committed
Christian, he does not just add one or two new practices on
to his old way of life. He becomes a new being. Christianity
is a new coat, not an old coat with a new patch. It is new

wine in a new bottle. The gospel is concerned with conversion and new birth. 'When a man becomes a Christian
he becomes a new creation. He is not the same. Everything
becomes new.' (2 Corinthians 5:17.) It is important that we
should not tone down this concept. We are called to sur-
render old prejudices, old passions, old fears, old conceits, old
negativities of body, mind and spirit. We are called to say –
'Come Lord Jesus, come Holy Spirit, begin the work of
new creation in me.' This work of new creation is of the
essence of Christian healing. We ought to be able actually to
feel it in body, mind and spirit. If as you and I look back
over the last twelve months we can see no evidence of new
creation, new growth, new Christian dimensions in ourselves, then we should ask ourselves seriously whether something is wrong with our understanding of the faith or with
the reality of our commitment to Christ.

The last verse of Luke 5 is a difficult one. It seems to con-
tradict all that has gone before. 'No one who has drunk old
wine wants new wine because he says, "The old wine is
good." ' Mark and Matthew leave the verse out. So do some
manuscripts of Luke's gospel. But the words could well go
back to Jesus. He went about doing the work of new creation,
but he well understood those who would not receive that
which he had to give. The verse forms a bridge between
chapters 5 and 6, where we meet Pharisees who were so preoccupied with the law of Moses that they would not receive
the gospel of Christ.

'Jesus was walking through some wheat fields on a sabbath
day. His disciples began to pick the heads of wheat, rub
them in their hands and eat the grain. Some of the Pharisees
said, "Why are you doing what our law says you must not
do on the sabbath?" ' They were objecting to a piece of
technical sabbath-breaking. Jesus had fallen foul of religious
conservatism, the attitude which says, 'We can't possibly do
this or that because we have never done it before.'

Jesus took the objection very seriously. He takes us all
seriously whether we deserve it or not. He said, 'Have you
not read what David did when he and his men were hungry?
He went into the house of God and took the consecrated
bread to eat and gave it to his men, though only the priests

are allowed to eat it.' And he added, 'The Son of Man is Lord even over the sabbath.' He was saying two things here. First, there have always been changes, even in King David's day. Secondly, the basic principle for keeping the sabbath is not that of religious conservatism but the lordship of the Son of Man, and by the Son of Man Jesus meant himself! What a claim – 'I am Lord even over the sabbath!' Only God incarnate could say such a thing. People had to make up their minds about him. What was he? Was he a blasphemous megalomaniac? Or was it conceivable that his authority was genuine and that actual Godhead was to be discerned in him? That is the great question which hovers over the pages of the gospels. It is a crucial question which still confronts the world today.

Luke's narrative continues with another story in which the observation of the sabbath is an ingredient. 'On another sabbath, Jesus went into the synagogue and taught. A man was there whose right hand was crippled. The lawyers and the Pharisees were on the watch to see whether Jesus would cure him on the sabbath, so that they could have a charge to bring against him.' What a state of mind! They did not seem to care about the man with the crippled hand, but as we see from so many parts of the world today it is so easy for bigotry to drive out both compassion and common sense. 'Jesus knew their thoughts,' – better than they did – 'and said to the man with the crippled hand, "Stand up and come to the front." ' The standing up and coming forward were not without significance. In our healing services there is two-fold symbolism. The coming forward symbolizes our availability to Jesus, the laying on of hands symbolizes his availability to us. So in the gospel-story the crippled man 'got up and stood there'. And Jesus said to the Pharisees, 'Here's a question for you. Which is the right thing? To do good on the sabbath? Or to do evil? To save life? Or to destroy it?' Jesus was still striving to reach out and communicate with them. He knew that there were two types of cripple present, the man who was crippled by a maimed hand and the Pharisees who were crippled by prejudice. He wanted healing for all, but on this occasion he had to be satisfied with a single physical healing. There was sullen silence from the lawyers and Pharisees and so 'when Jesus had looked round at them all, he said to the man, "Stretch out your hand." He did so and his hand was healed.'

It appears to have been an instantaneous healing. We see it happen in that way sometimes at our own services. I think of 'Janice' who had suffered from arthritis of the neck and head for years, till instantaneously at one of our services the pain vanished and has not recurred since; or 'Freda' who could not raise one of her arms above her shoulder before one of our services, but could wave it above her head afterwards; or 'Samantha' whose leg was numb following an operation, till feeling returned during one of our services. But these are exceptions. More often the healing reported to us is a more gradual process. Still, perhaps greater faithfulness and obedience to Jesus on our part would lead to a greater number of instantaneous healings. The implication of scripture is certainly that in the presence of Christ healing could happen very quickly indeed.

The story has a sad ending. The lawyers and Pharisees 'were filled with rage and began to discuss among themselves what they could do to harm Jesus'. We do not remain static after an encounter with Jesus. We find ourselves moving one way or another, towards him or away from him. The Jewish lawyers and ecclesiastics moved further and further away from him, and their hostility steadily increased, till they were obsessed with plots for his murder. Yet such is the wisdom of God that he used even that murder – in fact supremely that murder – for the healing of the souls of men.

However, that murder was still some distance away. In the meantime Jesus had much to do – much healing, much teaching, and much praying. We sometimes forget the importance to Jesus of prayer, but Luke was well aware of its centrality in his life and ministry. Following his encounter with the Pharisees we are told that he 'went up a hill to pray and spent the whole night praying to God'. Then equipped and strengthened by prayer, he made what was to be a crucial decision. 'When day came he called his disciples to him and selected twelve of them. He called them apostles. They were Simon (to whom he gave the name Peter), Andrew his brother, James and John, Philip and

Bartholomew, Matthew and Thomas, James the son of Alphaeus and Simon (known as 'the freedom fighter'), Judas the son of James and Judas Iscariot – his future betrayer.'

What an odd assortment! If we had been commissioned to choose twelve men whose leadership, wisdom and courage was to be a fundamental ingredient in God's plan to save the world we would never have made a choice like this. They were not a particularly well educated group. The first four were fishermen. They did not form a natural circle of friends. Matthew had collected taxes for the Romans and so would be regarded as a natural enemy by Simon, the freedom fighter, who had sworn to kill all who co-operated with Rome! They proved far from infallible. Peter denied Jesus. Thomas doubted Jesus. Judas betrayed Jesus.

So what was Jesus doing? He was doing what God always does. He was using the material at hand. He was refusing to force or manipulate human freedom. No doubt it would have been useful to have the High Priest amongst the apostles and the Roman Governor too. But the High Priest and the Roman Governor were not available. There were 'not many intellectuals, not many men of power, not many aristocrats' who were committed to the Carpenter of Nazareth. So God chose 'the foolish to confound the wise, the weak to confound the strong' (1 Corinthians 1:26–27). And he saw in those he called potentialities of which nobody else would have dreamed.

It is very consoling when you and I consider our local church. What if the smart set of the neighbourhood stay away? What if there is a dearth of rich or influential members? What if it is not a fashionable or culturally desirable parish? What if the people who do come to church are ill-assorted and nondescript? Then our situation is just about on the level with that of Jesus!

See what he did with his unlikely group. He had a two-stage plan. In Mark's account of the call of the Twelve he spells the plan out for us. Jesus ordained the Twelve first *'that they should be with him'* and then *'that he might send them out'* (Mark 3:14). Do we see these two elements in our own lives? Do we take time simply to be with Jesus? Are we conscious of his promise 'where two or three are gathered in my name, there am I in the midst?' Do we keep stillness in his presence – not an empty stillness but a stillness of awareness, receptiveness and obedience? And when he sends us out, then are we ready to go?

This is all highly relevant to Christian healing, because to be available to Christ's presence is to learn of his healing purposes and to receive his healing touch, and to be sent out by him is to take that same healing influence into the world. It is no accident that the first thing which happened to the Twelve after their ordination was that 'Jesus brought them down the hill to a level place where there was a large company of his followers. A great crowd of people had come from all over Judea and from Jerusalem and from the coastal cities of Tyre and Sidon. They came to hear him and to be healed of their diseases. Those who were troubled by unclean spirits were also healed. The whole crowd was trying to touch him. Healing power was radiating from him, affecting everybody.' (Luke 6:17–19.)

And there we leave him. Or rather we do no such thing! I am writing these words on an Easter Monday. Yesterday I was reminding my congregation that Christian worship is not just a commemoration of a dead hero, it is a meeting with a risen living Lord and Saviour, who with our consent will make all the difference in the world to us – and through us to the world. He is the same yesterday, today and for ever. He stands before us with the same loving gaze. He stands before us radiating the same healing power. He stands before us with the same authority and intent to cast out any evil which mars us. He offers the same commission. 'Be with me. Then go for me. Let my healing hands be upon you. Then be my healing hands in the world!'

May I conclude this chapter by offering you another simple method of healing prayer? It is based on the practice of the presence of the living Christ.

(1) Remember that Jesus is with you. 'Lo, I am with you always, even to the end of the world.' He looks at you and you look at him. His gaze is full of love for you, not sentimental, indulgent love but realistic, costly, saving love, of the sort that we thought about in chapter seven.

(2) That love is radiant and vibrant with God's own healing and recreating power. Picture and feel his hands upon you. Know that his will is for your wholeness.

(3) Now he looks straight into you. He sees clearly all that spoils and hurts you, any sin, any negativity, any evil or alien element. He rebukes it with God's own authority, and says, 'Come out of him,' 'Come out of her.' Let Christ have his way. Try not to resist. He only casts out that which is harmful or worthless. Do not protect it against him. The forces of evil must retreat before him unless we give them sanctuary.

(4) Now his hands are on you for healing again, because maybe the ministry of deliverance was painful for you. Let his love and joy and peace flow about you and into you, stirring God's own life in your body, mind and spirit.

(5) Now bring into his healing presence any for whom you wish to pray. You do not have to do anything. Just stand by, as Jesus looks at your friend, your neighbour, your loved one. Quietly and confidently align your will with that of his, as he speaks and touches the one for whom you are praying.

(6) Finally his eyes and his hands are back upon you. It is his will to send you into the world on his behalf. He has something for you to do and to be and his hands are upon you for commissioning, for empowering, for the gift of the Holy Spirit so that you may have whatever resources are needful.

Go in peace and serve the Lord. In the name of Christ. Amen.

CHAPTER TWELVE

Death of a Christian

A book on Christian healing could easily consist of case-history after case-history in which men, women and children who have become ill receive tangible physical benefit from the ministry of healing. Even in my own experience so many people have been completely or partially healed in this way that it stretches my credulity to breaking point to suggest that each of these instances is no more than coincidence. But any book which refers only to case-histories in which the ministry of healing is followed by a physical cure would be presenting less than the whole picture. The fact is that though often Christian healing 'works' at a physical level, there are many other cases where it does not do so.

Honesty and balance require that I should tell you such a story now, and that I should do so with equal care and equal emphasis to that given to the incidents about which we have already thought where physical healing did take place.

So may I introduce you to Jim Jordan, who was one of the two men whom I found serving the parish as lay readers when I arrived in Prenton? Jim was an intelligent and able man in his middle fifties. He worked as manager of the computer programming department at a large oil company. He was married with three sons, one of whom serves as our organist and choirmaster. He was a deep and thoughtful Christian, Methodist by upbringing but subsequently becoming a moderately high-church Anglican. Over the years he had come to occupy a central place in the life of the church in Prenton. In 1968 he became a reader and was found to have quite remarkable talent in the sensitive conduct of worship.

When I became Vicar of Prenton I was thrilled by the excellence of Jim's preaching and by the literary and spiritual

beauty of the prayers he composed for our worship Sunday
by Sunday. Here for instance is a typical prayer composed by
Jim.

We pray for the nations of the world and especially our
own nation: Father in heaven, whose will it is that all men
should worship you in the fellowship of the church and
serve you in the life of the world; send down upon our
nation a true spirit of repentance for the sinfulness which
passes for broadmindedness, the apathy which calls itself
tolerance, the materialism which glories in its prosperity
and grasps for more. And with this sorrow, O Lord God,
let faith and obedience go hand in hand, that men's lives
may be transformed and that integrity and godliness may
characterize our people, to your praise and honour. Amen.

Jim regarded the ministry of healing with some suspicion
when I first introduced it at St. Stephen's. He was afraid that
it might be distastefully emotional and theologically un-
sound. However, he weighed the issues and sifted the argu-
ments, and one Sunday I knew he had decided that the
ministry of healing was sound and good when before a healing service he took a taper and lit the altar candles. They are
usually lit only for communion services and not for evensong,
and this was Jim's way of saying that he now recognized the
centrality and the rightness of our service of Christian healing. Whether or not it is liturgically correct, we still have
the candles lit at that service. Shortly afterwards he agreed
to assist in the administration of the laying on of hands when
asked to do so.

After I had been in the parish for some time I was de-
lighted to find that Jim was seriously considering taking an
early retirement from his work as a computer programmer
and offering himself for the ministry. His wife, Jean, was
wholeheartedly with him in this.

Then at the beginning of 1977 Jim had a sudden heart
attack. He was rushed into hospital but seemed gradually
to recover and was discharged. He wrote in the parish
magazine to the people of the church – 'Thank you for your
concern, your messages, your cards, your gifts, your visits, and

most of all for your prayers during my illness. Jean and I
have been uplifted by your care. As to progress, I do just
that. I gather that my attack was fairly mild and if I am
sensible I should make a complete recovery.'

When he returned to us his preaching was better than ever
and his sense of vocation to the ministry was now very strong.
He offered himself to the Bishop of Chester as an ordinand
and was accepted. It was arranged that he should retire from
the oil firm the same summer and start at a theological
college in October.

But it was not to be. As he came to the point of retirement
a second heart attack took him into hospital again. My
colleagues and I visited him there and used every means we
knew to bring the ministry of healing to him. We laid on
hands. We anointed him. Regularly and frequently he received the sacrament of Holy Communion in his bed in the
hospital. Both inside the parish and outside it a great volume
of prayer went up for him. In hospital he received intensive
medical care. But it was all to no avail. He had a further
massive heart attack and though his consultant was in the
ward at the time and every possible aid was given to him,
Jim died almost immediately.

The church and the parish were stunned and shocked. So
were our Bishops and the Diocesan Director of Ordinands
who told me that he had regarded Jim as one of the most
talented and promising men in his care.

We were just on the eve of broadcasting from St. Stephen's
on the BBC World Service and Jim had written two prayers
specially for the broadcast. We felt it right still to use those
prayers in the broadcast, read by Jim's fellow reader, and so
these were Jim's last public words —

O Risen Christ,
Whose wounds declare the suffering and the victory of
    God,
We thank you for bursting the bonds of death.
Look at us now,
Look at *our* bonds,
Look at the things which tie us down,
Which fasten our hands and hobble our feet,

Which stop us from walking in your ways,
Which stop us from doing your works,
Which tether us so tightly to the dead weight of past
    failures,
And as you have burst the bonds of death,
So burst our bonds and set us free.
Set us free from our pride, set us free from our sin,
Set us free from our fear, set us free from ourselves.
Stand in our midst. Lay on us your hands. Breathe into
    us your breath,
So may the fire of your life fall upon us that we may
    have the faith to move the mountains of irrelevance in
    our churches, and may have that love without which
    faith is vain.
So give us speech that each man may hear us speak in his
    own tongue.
So give us life that we may create an army of disciples
    which can win the world for you.
Look at us Lord . . . and may this body be filled with your
    Spirit,
For your glory, for our peace, for the world and for your
    own sake. Amen.

Father in heaven,
Everything we have, all that we are comes from you, O
Lord. Every gift, every talent, all our potential are only
ours because they come direct from you. Lord, help us
not to belittle these gifts of yours, not to bury our talents,
but help us to use our time putting our talents to your
service, that we may carry your Son to the people of our
neighbourhood and to the people of the world.

Make us cheerful givers of these gifts as we use them
to your service and may we finally hear your accolade –
'Well done, good and faithful servant, enter into the joy
of your Master.'

All this we ask for the sake of Jesus Christ our Lord.
Amen.

There could, I suppose, be no finer last word on the life of
any man. But why did this have to be Jim's last word? Why

was a life which promised to do so much for God and man cut short? Why when Christian healing so often works such wonders did it not work for Jim? We often talk grandly of the Christian conquest of death. But what meaning can it have in the light of the death of Jim Jordan?

CHAPTER THIRTEEN

The Conquest of Death

Death is a very personal subject. One day you and I will die and before that we shall probably suffer the pangs of bereavement on a number of occasions. If Christianity is a true and comprehensive religion it must deal with the subject of death directly and unflinchingly.

It was, in fact, one of the things which the ancient world found most remarkable about the early Christian church that in a society which was obsessed with the fear of death, Christians seemed to have no such fear. Even when Christianity was declared an illegal religion punishable by death, many Christians made death their deliberate choice rather than deny their Lord and their faith.

As St. Athanasius wrote – 'It is natural for man to fear death and the dissolution of the body, but it is a most remarkable fact that the man who has accepted the faith of the cross scorns this natural emotion and for the sake of Christ does not fear death.'

Of course death, unlike disease, is not necessarily contrary to God's will for us. He has made us physically finite. Though my earthly body is precious to God, it is his will that one day I shall discard it.

What effect then does the ministry of Christian healing have upon death and dying? There seem to be three possibilities.

First because Christian healing so often results in physical improvements there are certainly occasions when an impending death is averted. 'Alfred' was dying, so I was told when I visited him in hospital, but after prayer and the laying on of hands in the name of the Lord he made a complete recovery and is still alive many years later. 'Emma' was supposed to have terminal cancer, but she told me that

the Lord had appeared to her in a dream and told her she
would not die. He gave her a simple action to perform –
rather like Naaman washing in the River Jordan (2 Kings
5:10) – and she did it obediently and trustingly. To the
astonishment of her consultant the cancer vanished without
trace. She is still alive many years later. 'Stanley' was bed-
fast and he and his wife thought he was dying, but following
a laying on of hands he was up and about the house within
hours! 'Delia' was in a coma when I visited her in hospital.
The ward sister had little hope for her and her family were
worried to distraction about her. I prayed over and laid
hands upon her unconscious body. Next day she was conscious, alert and on the way to recovery and, in fact, she
became fitter than she had been for years!

However, we must turn back to Jim Jordan and recognize
that in a second category of ailments Christian healing produces little or no evidence of physical improvement and does
not avert death. In fact I actually believe that in certain
cases Christian healing may even accelerate death! I think
of 'Amy', a lovely gentle old lady whose body was wracked
with an advanced gas gangrene condition. She was in con-
tinuous pain and many would have died long before she
did, but as the doctor told her family, she had a strong and
vigorous heart and there seemed no prospect other than that
of weeks of continuing agony ahead of her. Her family
called me in. They told me that neither she, nor they, were
afraid of death. 'If only she could pass away quickly and
quietly . . . ' they said. I laid on hands in the Lord's name
and prayed for his healing intervention. Amy was dead
within hours. Or there was 'Judith' who had a brain tumour.
The doctor said she would live for about a fortnight, but it
would be a fortnight of agony. I laid on hands and prayed
and again she was dead within hours.

In Jim's case I see no evidence of an acceleration of death,
but neither was it averted, and to the story of Jim I could
add other instances of people for whom I have prayed and
longed for healing but in whom physical healing did not
take place and death was not averted.

Why should one man live and another man die? I just
do not know. All I could suggest when I faced this problem

in chapter 5 of *Christian Healing Rediscovered* was that

there are laws governing the universe; laws of logic, laws of nature, laws of life. We are beginning to have a better understanding of some of them but there is much to learn. God does not break these laws. They are part of his own nature. When we pray for physical healing and it does not happen, some factor within the laws of life is preventing it. There would be no failure of healing in a perfect world, but this sinful world is far from perfect and contains many a block to healing. Very often we cannot see where the block lies. It may not be in the sufferer at all. For myself I am sure that it never lies in God.

There is little more that I can add. Perhaps one can identify some of the blocks. Despair or rigidity of thought on the part of the sufferer, negativity of outlook on the part of friends and relatives, the sins and follies of society as a whole, and the church's lack of faith and obedience may be just a few. In many individual cases it may well be better not to try to work it out.

What God does, when his primary will for perfect wholeness of body, mind and spirit is frustrated for some reason, is to employ one of two alternative plans. One is to use the suffering productively and redemptively, and I believe that the other is to lead the sufferer, through death, to a healing beyond death.

Probably we make too much fuss about death. We treat it as though it were the great full stop at the end of the book of life, the ultimate loss, the ultimate defeat. Whereas if we take Jesus seriously, we should think of it as more like the turning of a page between one chapter and another, or as crossing a boundary between one country and another. The dying man is 'moving house'. I remember when we moved from Hyde to Prenton. There were some sad moments. There are people we miss and folk who miss us. And the moving process is a messy business, really rather a nuisance. We often said we wished we could somehow be moved without actually going through the struggles of moving. But it all worked out well enough and now we would not want to turn the clock back.

Dying must be something like that. Few people may actually enjoy it but if we go into it in the company of the Lord, with our trust in him and our hand in his hand, I believe we can go in peace and in confidence. Just as the company of Christ makes all the difference to this life, so I believe it will make a difference which this world could never imagine to that which lies beyond death. In the appendix at the end of this book I list some of the reasons why I believe it to be logical and right to believe that death is not the end. At Jim's funeral I felt impelled to say not just that I believe in eternal life as a general concept but that I believe in Jim's eternal life in particular. 'God so loved the world that he gave his only begotten Son, that whosoever believes in him should not perish but have everlasting life.' (John 3:16.) And Jim certainly believed in Jesus and longed for others to do so.

If Jim were looking over my shoulder as I write he would probably be having a quiet chuckle that I am making so much of what seems to me his untimely death. He was never a very fit man. He was often in pain, though he tried not to show it. Whereas now, if there is any truth in the Christian faith, Jim is fit and well and free and fulfilled, at home with his Lord.

That thought may seem to provide a fitting point to end this chapter on the Christian conquest of death, but earlier I mentioned three possibilities on the effect that Christian healing can have upon death and dying, and so far we have considered only two of them.

Jesus described his own healing ministry by saying, 'the blind see, the lame walk, the lepers are cleansed, the deaf hear, *the dead are raised*, the poor have the gospel preached to them', (Luke 7:22). Raising the dead was certainly not a common occurrence in his ministry, but the gospels tell us that it did happen on rare occasions, for instance when earlier in the same chapter of Luke the only son of a widow was raised from the dead (Luke 7:11–18). When Jesus commended the healing ministry to his disciples he did not exclude the raising of the dead. In fact he specifically included it in the command to the apostles recorded in Matthew's gospel (10:8) – 'Heal the sick, raise the dead!'

Clearly we should not expect this to happen frequently, if the ministry of Jesus sets the pattern, but it would seem that it is something which can and does still happen, as for instance in the strange story of Captain Edmund Wilbourne of the Church Army, who visits our parish from time to time because it is his work to supervise the Church Army's parochial work.

Captain Wilbourne was prevailed upon to tell this story in an interview with the Rev. Eddie Neale, broadcast on BBC Radio Merseyside early in 1976. It is I think the most remarkable radio interview I have ever heard. Captain Wilbourne has given me his permission to reproduce it, so that you can judge for yourself. The events it describes took place back in 1949. So we have no momentary resurrection here. Edmund Wilbourne is still very much alive and active.

Without more ado, let us turn to that radio interview. Here, slightly edited, is a transcript.

Eddie Neale: Last week someone telephoned me and put me in touch with a Church Army Captain who claims that he died while in hospital. He lives in London now, but I gave him a ring just before the programme and asked him to tell me the story.

Edmund Wilbourne: Well, it's a strange story. It's not one that I really like to talk about because sometimes the deepest things of our lives are rather hard to put into words. The reason I come to be talking to you about it at all is that last year I went to Wigan on a Church Army Mission and I met there a young couple whose son had been tragically killed. So I spoke to them and told them this to comfort and to help them, and I presume somehow or other the story has got back to you. It happened some time ago. I had pneumonia and pleurisy and was taken to the Crumpsall Hospital near Manchester and I actually died.

E.N.: You were clinically dead, were you?

E.W.: Yes, that's right, preparations were made for my burial. I can picture the scene. I saw myself lying on the bed. I saw a young nurse. I remember thinking at the time how young she was to have to do such a thing as getting me ready and even shaving me.

E.N.: You saw this? What do you mean, you saw it?

E.W.: I actually saw it taking place – I was detached from it, it was as if I was there watching and I was the third party. I felt no emotion, no elation, just nothing – just a picture, it was almost as if a cord linked myself to my body on the bed.

E.N.: You were detached from your body looking at yourself.

E.W.: Yes, as if I couldn't go. I thought I was caught there, and then it seemed as if the cord was severed and I arrived at a place. It's very hard to put this into words but I can only describe it as heaven, a place of activity, nothing like floating on clouds or harps or anything of that sort. I recognized people.

E.N.: Was it nice?

E.W.: It was a wonderful feeling. In fact I felt more alive and more alert than I've ever done since, or ever did before. It almost seemed, too, as if the pieces of a jig-saw all fitted together. You know how it is with a tapestry, how you see the back of a tapestry and all the interwoven parts, and when the tapestry's turned over you see how it all fits into place. Suddenly I saw how all my life fitted together to that point. I could have been there for ever and ever, and I saw Jesus Christ. I was aware of him by the print of the nails in his hands and his feet, and I remember I was very amused, I thought it was a joke at the time – it made me laugh, and other people laughed with me; I think there must be humour in heaven. I said 'You know, these are the only man-made things in heaven.' I thought it was wildly funny. I don't know why, but it just appealed to me at that time particularly.

E.N.: Yes.

E.W.: Because of my relationship to him and the way that he looked at me, I knew that there was no need to worry or to be afraid.

E.N.: How long were you actually supposed to be dead?

E.W.: About two hours, which is quite some considerable

time – at least it was then. I don't know whether there's been another record established since then.

E.N.: No, it certainly is. And how were you revived?

E.W.: Well again in this state I heard as it were a whisper, which got louder and louder, of an elderly woman's voice praying, 'O God don't let him die, O God don't let him die, O God don't let him die, he's got a work for you to do.' This grated and I didn't like it at all, and the Lord Jesus turned me round on my shoulder and gave me a gentle push and said something to the effect 'It's not time for you yet,' and I woke up in the mortuary of Crumpsall Hospital and it was the Mortuary Attendant who nearly had a heart attack!

E.N.: A lot of people, of course, would say that this was some form of dream.

E.W.: Yes they would.

E.N.: What would your reaction be to that?

E.W.: I'm well aware of that. All I know is that it's made all the difference to my life.

E.N.: In what way?

E.W.: You can't take it from me. It's given me a purpose and a joy and a determination to tell other people – not about this, but about the Lord Jesus Christ. I don't talk about this very much, because I'm so afraid that people will perhaps think I'm a crank or a liar, so one keeps it to oneself. It was a long time later that I found that at the moment that I actually died my elderly landlady who was there, knelt down by the side of my bed and prayed, 'O don't let him die, O don't let him die, he's got a work for you to do.'

A similar interview was subsequently broadcast on the magazine programme *Sunday* on BBC Radio 4. Afterwards Captain Wilbourne received over five hundred letters from listeners who wished to ask further questions. Most of them were from young people rather than from the elderly, and the BBC agreed to provide secretarial help and to pay the postage so that each of these could receive an answer.

After hearing both interviews I found I had a variety of supplementary questions of my own, and Captain Wilbourne kindly agreed to see me and answer them.

First I asked him how he could be sure that he was actually clinically dead during his lost two hours. He answered that although thirty years after the event it would be difficult to trace the medical documentation, nobody seemed to have had any doubt about it at the time. His death certificate was written out and signed, and his body was moved to the mortuary. His first job after his resuscitation was to try to comfort the mortuary attendant, who was in a state of some shock after seeing the 'body' sit up on the mortuary slab! Afterwards Captain Wilbourne was told that he had made medical history, but from his own point of view the question of whether or not he was clinically dead was less important than his certainty that he had been permitted to have a foretaste of heaven.

I asked him to tell me more about this experience of heaven. What was heaven like? What effect did it have on him? Who were the people he recognized? What were they like? Did they have physical shape? And in particular what was Jesus like and how did he recognize him?

Heaven, he said, was a place of intense light, a place of intense activity, more like a bustling city than a lonely country scene. While he was there he felt 'at the centre of things'. For himself being there was both enlightening and cleansing. He felt he could see the point of life. Everything fitted in. It all made sense. His own life made sense – even the dark times. The only jarring element was a sense of irritation and regret that he had not told more people about Jesus. There was no sense of time. In a way it seemed as though everyone dies at the same time, and so heaven is a great reunion experience.

Edmund Wilbourne says that our normal spatio-temporal vocabulary is frustratingly inadequate to describe heaven. However, if one cannot speak meaningfully in terms of time and space, one can come closer to doing so in terms of relationship and recognition. 'The people I recognized whilst dead were my mother and grandmother, and although I could not have recognized them, I was aware of such giants as Peter and Paul and the founder of the Church Army, Wilson Carlile. There were also numerous Christian people

I have known in life. I especially recognized a Sunday
School teacher called Frank, who influenced me a great deal
and who lost his life in the second world war. I think that I
was surrounded by what I can only describe as a reception
committee. Frank was one of these. Another was my saintly
Roman Catholic doctor, who had just previously died.
These are the people who enjoyed my "joke". They did have
physical shape. It is hard to describe, but it somehow combined the youth and vigour of a twenty-one year old with
a sense of perfect maturity.'

As for Jesus, in that place of light Jesus was 'light itself'.
This does not mean he was an abstraction. He was as much
'a person' as all the others. He was prophet, priest and king.
'I knew him by the nail-holes in his hands and feet – and by
the way he looked at me. I shall never forget the look of
Jesus. It was a searching look which saw every part of me,
but I realized that he could not take his eyes off me because
he loved me so.'

This *love* is the major impression which Edmund Wilbourne still retains. In heaven, he says, there is light, peace,
music, beauty, and joyful activity, but above all there is
love, and within this love he felt truly alive, as he had never
been before. Captain Wilbourne was reluctant to be prayed
back to the lesser life of this earth, but he sees his return as
having purpose. He feels that, as his old landlady said in her
prayer, he has 'got a work to do for God'. He was strongly
aware during his visit to heaven that his relationship with
the heavenly Lord stemmed from the fact that on earth he
had accepted Jesus as Saviour. Now he has reapplied himself to the work of a Church Army evangelist with a new
urgency, a new authority, a new sense of commission to proclaim Jesus Christ as 'the way, the truth and the life' both
in time and in eternity.

The God Within

It may seem that any chapter following the story of a man
raised from the dead must be something of an anti-climax,
but I believe that the theme of the present chapter is in
fact even more extraordinary.

'I believe in the Holy Spirit.' I say so every Sunday, and so
do my congregation. But I wonder how many of us have
really paused to work out the enormity of the doctrine we
are professing and of the claim we are making?

If you and I are prepared to say that we believe in the
Holy Spirit, the third person of the Holy Trinity, we are
saying that we do not just believe in the Creator God who
is the ground and source of all creation, known and unknown, we do not just believe that in a remarkable way
God's true nature has been revealed to us in the life and
death and essence of our Saviour Jesus Christ, we are also
saying that we believe in our own capacity for oneness with
Godhead.

The devil is always telling us that the Christian faith has a
low doctrine of self. 'Come to me,' he says, 'and I will give
you a proper sense of your own importance. Stay away from
Jesus or he'll have you grovelling in no time, because to be
a Christian is to be self-depreciatory and self-contemptuous.'

The truth is in fact the very opposite. If you are interested
in the lowest possible concept of the value of man, then go
to the devil! While it is true that the devil encourages self-
centredness, the self-centredness he most favours is a strange
mixture of self-conceit and self-contempt. It is miles away
from genuine self-respect. Often it cannot bear to look at
itself honestly and survives only by pretence and self-delusion.
And the devil is not called 'the destroyer' for nothing. The
paths of sin are the paths of self-destruction. Think of a sin –

hate, lust, greed, jealousy, any sin at all. Do not attitudes like these self-evidently diminish the human spirit and in the last resort threaten to destroy it?

By contrast, if it is a high concept of man you are after, try the gospel. True, the gospel tells me I need to be cleansed from my sins, but this is not because I am worthless, it is because I am too precious to stay uncleansed. If I wash my body when it becomes dirty, it is not because my body is unimportant to me but because I think it worth caring for. If when I sustain a physical injury or sickness, I send for a doctor, it is because my body is too important for me to allow sickness to go untreated. Similarly the concern of the Christian gospel that Christ should minister to the sickness of my soul is a sign of the value that my Father puts upon me.

God made each one of us in his own image. Each one of us constitutes a walking miracle just by existing, and as for our ultimate potential, words cannot express it. We have marred this image by our sin and stupidity, but God is not defeated. We have a Saviour. By crib and cross God has shared our nature that we might share his. And from the Father and the Son proceeds the Holy Spirit, the God within, by whom and for whom we were made, the God who is our deepest nature, our truest self.

What difference does it make if we really believe in the God within? It makes, quite literally, all the difference in the world. The concept of the God within is not just a doctrine but the basis for a host of practicalities, as is always the case with Christian theology.

Consider for instance the implication of this concept for Christian conduct. It must make a difference to my dealing with my neighbour if I have some hint of his divinity or at least his potentiality for divinity.

Consider too its implication for those occasions when we are targets for some sort of temptation. Satan's blandishments must surely seem less attractive if we have a firm grasp upon the Christian concept of selfhood. Think of yourself – created as you are in God's image, loved all the way to the cross by Jesus, and designed to be one with God's own Holy Spirit. There is no improving on that for a destiny. To hang the devil's tawdry trappings about such a creature would be as senseless as taking a necklace of priceless pearl and spraying it with cheap gaudy paint!

And of course true belief in the Holy Spirit must logically have the most profound effect on our approach to Christian healing. If my own deep nature is that of the God within, then ailments of body, mind and spirit are out of place and can have no more than a passing foothold. To stir the Spirit in ourselves and in others must be a powerful act of healing.

So may I offer you a further method of healing prayer? We have already thought of a method of healing prayer based on an awareness of the peace of God the Father and a second method based on the practice of the presence of God the Son, our Lord Jesus Christ. Here now is a meditation on the healing work of God the Holy Spirit.

(1) Recollect the promise of Jesus – 'Your Heavenly Father *will* give the Holy Spirit to those who ask him,' (Luke 11:13).

(2) All who put their faith in Jesus as Lord and Saviour may and should claim this promise. Otherwise our Christianity will be tragically incomplete. The gift of the Holy Spirit has been God's deep purpose for us since our creation. 'God has shared our manhood that we might share his Godhead,' (Athanasius). Jesus promised his disciples – 'The Holy Spirit will be in you,' (John 14:17). Just as being a Christian involves taking God the Father on trust from Jesus, equally it involves taking on trust from him God the Holy Spirit. So here and now, simply and trustingly, claim the promise of the Holy Spirit. If in your own life you have decided Jesus is to be trusted then his promise of the Holy Spirit is also to be trusted. Claim the promise. Thank God for the fact of the Holy Spirit in *you*.

(3) As with wonder you recollect the God within, remember that the Holy Spirit is the Lord and giver of life. Feel and enjoy the life of God surging in you. Make a mental act of assent and co-operation with the life of God in you – the life of God stirring in every cell of the body, the life of God sharpening and enlightening your mind, the life of God fitting your spirit for eternal life. The God within is your true self, the *yóu* that God envisaged since the beginning of time. Say yes to your true self.

(4) The life of God in you stirs and moves with God's own strength and God's own goodness. Picture the life of God in you, gently but inevitably nudging aside all that is in you which is alien to your true self, all that hurts or spoils your body, mind or spirit. Relax and let the God within have his way with you.

(5) The life of God within you is one with the ring of peace around you and the healing Lord who has introduced you to both Father and Spirit. Also the Holy Spirit in you is one with the Holy Spirit in those who are around you. Recollect Jesus's prayer to the Father for all believers – 'that they may be one, just as we are one, I in them and you in me, that in this oneness they may be made perfect' (John 17:22–23). Pray for the church of God, that it may be active and alive by its oneness with the Holy Spirit. Picture your own church being led by the Holy Spirit into life and love and truth and healing power. Offer this mental picture to God in simple trust that it may be so in the Lord's name. Picture the life of God in every person for whom you feel called to pray. There is no person to whom the life of God is completely alien. Thank God that his life is good, and again in simple trust pray that God may have his own healing and saving way in all his creatures.

(6) Finally wait upon the Holy Spirit in silence for some moments. The Father has something for you to do and to be. The Holy Spirit in you is one with the Father and knows his will for you. And with that knowledge he has the necessary gifts and resources for that will to be done through you. Be still and know the purpose and the power of the kingdom of God within you.

(7) Then go in the power of that same Holy Spirit – who is both true God and your true self. Touch the world for healing.

CHAPTER FIFTEEN

Invitation to Christian Healing

The purpose of this book is not just to present a point of view but to pass on an invitation.

Jesus said –

'Those who believe will lay hands on the sick and healing will take place,' (Mark 16:18). Many a startled believer has found it to be true. One of the reviewers of my former book told me of an incident of healing which illustrates this. At the time when he was reading the book to review it he was off work in bed with an unpleasant dose of influenza. The book's line of thought seemed basically sound to him and so it struck him as logical that he should try it out for himself. He sent for the local Curate and asked for prayer for healing and a laying on of hands in the name of the Lord. The Curate said he was not accustomed to the ministry of healing but that he was prepared to do what was asked. The result was an unexpectedly rapid departure of the influenza, a return to work well ahead of schedule, a somewhat bewildered Curate – and a favourable book review!

A year ago one of our neighbouring parishes instituted a mid-week service of healing with the laying on of hands. Some months ago the Vicar told me this remarkable story. A local couple who longed for a baby but had been childless for eight years asked for a service of healing to bring God's power and love to the condition of childlessness. The service was arranged, and it was agreed that it should also be a proxy form of ministration and prayer for the husband's father who was in hospital with a cancer condition in which a lung was collapsed. (There was also a probability of secondary growths in the brain.) Husband and wife received prayer, laying on of hands and anointing. With a startling speed the wife found she was having a baby (a boy, as it turned out) and within days of the service father's lung reflated and an X-ray could find no trace of any cancer whatsoever! My colleague tells me he is conscious of no specialist gift of healing. He says – 'I just try to obey the gospel orders!'

There seems little doubt that a similar awareness of gospel orders is today leading more and more to an involvement in the ministry of Christian healing. Whether they are high, low or middle in their churchmanship seems not to matter. With increasing frequency letters come to me asking for prayer for this church or that because the members are just about to start services of healing. Of course there is more to the ministry of Christian healing than an occasional service and a periodic laying on of hands. Christian healing is a way of life, a way of love, a way of prayer, a way of expectant recognition that Jesus is the same yesterday, today and for ever. There is so much to ponder, so far to go. But 'a journey of a thousand miles begins with a single step'. Whenever a group of Christians take that step, or when even a single individual does so, the kingdom of God comes a little nearer.

What then can you and I do to respond to Jesus's invitation to identify ourselves with him in his healing work? We can all undertake healing prayer of a sort similar to that described earlier in the book. If we incorporate it into our daily prayers, we shall inevitably be the better for it ourselves, and others too will feel the benefit.

However, perhaps you are in a position to do more than this. Perhaps you can bring the challenge of the ministry of healing to the notice of your local church. If so why not? It is a comprehensive ministry, relevant to men's wholeness at every level of body, mind and spirit, relevant to the problems and potentialities of neighbourhoods and nations. It is a logical ministry – true to human reason, so far as reason goes, and rooted in much experience. It is a responsible ministry, for it takes the concept of the church as the body of Christ seriously and recognizes that his work must be our work. It is a scriptural ministry because a Bible from which all reference of healing had been expurgated would be no more than shreds and fragments. It is a ministry of exploration and rediscovery – much needed where the church is stagnant. It is a stretching and challenging ministry, much needed where the church is complacent. It is a ministry of close union with the Lord, much needed where the church is worldly. It is a ministry through which the power of God can be discerned and unleashed, but is nonetheless within the reach of ordinary Christians and ordinary churches.

It is not a heretical ministry because it does not spring from any novelty of doctrine but, as we have seen, it is firmly founded upon belief in God the Father, God the Son and God the Holy Spirit. It is not a presumptuous ministry because it makes us continually subordinate to the Lord's word and dependent upon his saving power.

The invitation to Christian healing comes from no less a source than Jesus himself. It requires a response, like a card marked R.S.V.P. For centuries all too few have acknowledged this invitation, but it has never been withdrawn.

It comes to *you* now.

APPENDIX

Why Believe in Life after Death? –
A Tabulation of Evidence

(1) History teaches us that right from the beginning there has been an ingrained conviction in man that death is not the end. One of the earliest facts known about Stone-Age man is that he buried his dead, often with valuable tools, weapons and cooking utensils. Stone was used for sepulchres before it was used for houses. As man became vocal and coherent he pondered and elaborated upon this conviction and the great ancient religions and philosophies testify to this – the elaborate Egyptian death rituals, the Chinese concept of ancestor worship, the Japanese two-tiered after-life, Hinduism with its concept of the imperishable soul or *atma*, Buddhism with its noble eightfold path leading to *nirvana*, the Homeric concept of Hades, the Hebraic idea of Sheol, Plato's teaching on immortality, and so on.

The conviction that there is life after death is to be found throughout the world from the dawn of history. Where has it come from? Not, one would think, from wishful thinking. There is nothing desirable, for instance, about the Homeric Hades. Total oblivion would be much better. Is the notion of survival then rather a basic concept arising from the experience of life?

(2) There are various elements in man's normal experience which hint at life after death.

For instance there are many aspects of human nature which would be wasted if man were confined to his earthly years. We are aware of elements in us which cannot develop to the full if we have only our allotted span on earth to develop them. As Immanuel Kant put it, 'Man's faculties, desires and earthly gifts reach far beyond earthly use.'

Then too man's spirit can assert an independence of his

body, for instance in sickness or old age. Victor Hugo has written: 'You say that the soul is nothing but the resultant of bodily powers. Why then is my soul more luminous as the bodily powers begin to fail? Winter is on my head, but eternal spring is in my heart. The nearer I approach the end, the plainer I hear round me the immortal symphonies of the world to come.'

There is a hint in this quotation of something more – a mystical experience of eternity. This would appear to be not an uncommon phenomenon. C. S. Lewis writes about his personal experience of this in *Surprised by Joy* (pages 22–23). Rosalind Heywood writes of her experience in Arnold Toynbee's symposium *Man's Concern with Death* (pages 249–50). The apostle Paul wrote of a similar experience in 2 Corinthians 12:2–4. And of course for Jesus a personal awareness of eternity was part of the air he breathed and an integral element in his teaching.

(3) This brings me personally to my own primary reason for believing in life after death. In a world where archaeology, history, religion and literature hint time and time again of the existence of life after death – Jesus speaks plainly about it. He does not harp upon it. He is not preoccupied with it. But it is an essential strand in his basic teaching.

This is recorded by all four evangelists. For instance Matthew records Christ's injunction to 'lay up treasures in heaven' (Matthew 6:19–20); Mark records the promise that those who make sacrifices for the sake of Christ will receive 'in the world to come eternal life' (Mark 10:30); Luke tells us that the children of the resurrection 'cannot die any more: for they are equal to the angels and are the children of God' (Luke 20:36); and John preserves for us the assurance that 'God so loved the world that he gave his only begotten Son, that whosoever believes in him should not perish but have everlasting life,' (John 3:16).

Any reader wishing to study the teaching of Jesus on life after death in greater detail may find it helpful to look up these further texts – Mark 12:26–27 (Jesus refutes the Sadducees when they deny the resurrection); John 14:2 (the Father's 'many mansions'); Matthew 13:24–30; 36–43 (parable of the wheat and the tares); Matthew 25: 31–46 (parable of the sheep and the goats); John 11:25–26 ('I am the resurrection and the life . . . ').

In this sort of way Jesus taught about life after death throughout his years of ministry and continued to do so in the hour of his death when he turned to the penitent thief and said, 'Today you shall be with me in paradise,' (Luke 23:43).

So history is full of the conviction that there is life after death. The conviction is supported by various aspects of man's normal experience of himself and is amplified by some of the world's greatest teachers, prominent among whom is Jesus.

(4) In addition to all this there is a further sphere of human experience which is relevant to an enquiry into evidence for life after death. This is a type of experience which can hardly be called 'normal', though it is not unusual. The name 'paranormal' is therefore sometimes given to it.

Many have found this sphere an impressive source of evidence for life after death. For instance Professor C. D. Broad, formerly Knightbridge Professor of Moral Philosophy at Cambridge, who has made no secret of his own preference *not* to survive death, has nonetheless recorded the opinion that paranormal phenomena suggest persistence after death (*Lectures on Psychical Research*, page 430). The majority report of the commission set up by the Archbishops of Canterbury and York in 1937 to investigate this question came to the same conclusion.

Amongst the evidence which has to be weighed is the fact that many people have made the claim that they have been taken out of the body to other places in this world or beyond this world. This seems surprisingly common. Some years ago a survey was conducted among 350 undergraduates at Oxford, and 34 per cent claimed out-of-the-body experiences. In similar surveys the percentage at Duke University, North Carolina was 30 per cent, and that at Southampton University was 19 per cent. In my own ministry I have met people who have made the same claim. I think of 'Roger', a university lecturer, who told me that one day while lecturing to a group of students he found himself somehow separated from his body looking down upon the class from the back of

the room. With a real effort of will he pulled himself back
into his body. Throughout it all the lecture continued, and
as far as he could tell his students did not notice anything
amiss. There is a detailed description of a similar experience
(taken from an address given by Lord Geddes) in Arnold
Toynbee's *Man's Concern with Death* (pages 195–97). There
is a selection of other such experiences in Jack Winslow's
book *The Gate of Life* (pages 34–45).

Further evidence for consideration lies in the claim made
by a large number of people that they have experienced contact with someone from the far side of death. There is warn-
ing in the Bible that this sort of contact should not be sought
(Isaiah 8:19–20; Deuteronomy 18:10–12). But many say
that the contact can take place spontaneously. There is the
celebrated instance in which J. B. Phillips (in *Ring of Truth*,
pages 89–90) claims he was twice visited by C. S. Lewis
after his death. Rosalind Heywood relates a similar experience in *Man's Concern with Death* (page 244). Amongst
people I have met myself I think of 'Bernard', a widower
who tells me that his wife has visited him in clearly visible
form on half a dozen occasions, and 'Judith' a widow whose
husband comes to her occasionally in a form that is not only
visible but tangible, and 'Marguerite' an eminently sane and
practical-minded Christian woman who has a wide circle
of 'spirit' friends whose company she has come to enjoy
greatly.

(5) Related to the paranormal evidence but in some way
distinct from it there is the evidence which thanatologists are
collecting in increasing quantity about the experience of
dying. Various types of people are prepared to talk about
this experience. There are those who come very close to
death during illness or following severe illness, but subsequently recover. There are those who die, but whilst dying
tell those around them what they experience as they approach
death. And there are the strange experiences of those who
are actually pronounced dead but are resuscitated either
medically or in some other way. I think of 'Matthew' who
'died' on the operating table but was medically resuscitated.
He told me afterwards of his experience of leaving his body
and floating outwards. 'People I have known floated around

me and I tried to find someone whom I could hold on to,' he said, 'but they all evaded me, till Jesus came towards me and I found that I did not have to hold him. He held me!' The experience of Captain Edmund Wilbourne, recorded in chapter 14, is a further instance, and is remarkable for the length of time for which he had been 'dead'. Further instances are recorded in Dr Raymond Moody's book *Life after Life*, though perhaps along with it a book of a more critical nature should be read such as *Is There Life After Death?* by John Weldon and Zola Levitt, who warn their readers against the dangers of wishful thinking and even of 'demonic deception'.

(6) Similar to other paranormal happenings and yet in many ways unique is the raising of Jesus from the dead. Christians believe in this as a matter of faith, but quite apart from faith the objective evidence for the historicity of the resurrection of Jesus is very strong indeed.

There is no lack of non-biblical reference to it amongst writers in the eighty years which followed his death. The Epistle of Barnabas (dated soon after A.D. 70) refers to it. So does Flavius Josephus (or perhaps an early interpreter into his writings) round about or soon after A.D. 94. So does Clement, Bishop of Rome (writing in A.D. 96–97). So does Ignatius of Antioch, who died in A.D. 115. So does Ignatius's contemporary, Polycarp, Bishop of Smyrna.

The biblical evidence is earlier still. When Paul wrote about the resurrection appearances that Jesus made to Peter and to the Twelve and to a crowd of over five hundred people, to James on his own, to all the apostles, and finally to Paul himself (1 Corinthians 15:3–8) he was relying on eye-witnesses and was writing in A.D. 56. The things he said could be checked and exposed if they were wrong, just as I could be checked if I were to write about life in the second world war. In fact Paul was nearer to the resurrection of Jesus than we are to the second world war! And to the letters of Paul must be added the evidence of the four gospels, written later in the same century (only a few years later in the case of Mark).

Contemporaries who denied the Christian interpretation of events seemed not to deny the fact of the empty tomb and the stone rolled away. This in itself appears to point to the truth of the resurrection. The Christian claim that Jesus had risen from the dead may be hard to believe – but the alternative explanations which were suggested do not bear investigation at all. One cannot believe that the Christians moved the body and then went on to witness to and die for a fraud, or that the enemies of Jesus stole the body and then never thought to say so when the Christians were claiming a resurrection.

The eye-witnesses, the letters, the gospels, the moved stone are all powerful evidence. But more powerful still is the fact that there was a basic change on the part of the disciples after the resurrection. From a small group of beaten, bewildered, frightened people, huddling together in an upper room, they changed to a purposive and courageous company whose aim was to conquer the world for Christ. There were thousands of converts. And, when Christianity was declared an illegal religion punishable by death, thousands faced martyrdom. What made them do it? They said it was because they knew Christ was risen and so they did not fear death. Is there any other feasible explanation? I know of none. Human nature is intractable stuff. What other than the miracle of the resurrection could have changed it?

This summary covers just part of the evidence that Jesus rose from the dead. A lawyer with whom I recently discussed it ventured the opinion that the evidence for the resurrection would convince any court in the land!

In short a survey of past and present history, an investigation into normal and paranormal experience, and the teachings of many faiths in many lands, conjoin to produce a massive mountain of supportive evidence that life is not designed to terminate at the point of death. For Christians the word of Christ and the rising of Christ from the dead clinch the matter.

Of course hard upon the heels of the question, 'Is there life after death?' there press a host of further questions. What will it be like? Will all men experience it? Will all experience it in the same way? How may we prepare for it? What about heaven and hell?

What a frustrating point at which to end a book! But life's exploration is like that. As soon as one question begins to be answered another is instantly raised. However even in a final paragraph this at least can be said. If we are correct in believing that we can walk through this life without fear when we hold to the healing hand of Christ, trusting him as Lord and Saviour, it seems right and reasonable to suppose that holding the same healing hand we can also walk without fear into death, and through death, and into the mystery of whatever lies beyond. The New Testament and other early Christian documents have no doubt about it. So let them have the last word. 'For God so loved the world that he gave his only begotten Son that whosoever believes in him should not perish but have everlasting life.' 'God gives freely, and his gift is eternal life in union with Jesus Christ our Lord.' 'God has prepared for those who love him things beyond our seeing, things beyond our hearing, things beyond our imagining.' 'God has given us eternal life in his Son.' 'Know that you have eternal life, you who believe in the Son of God.' 'It is not clear what we shall become, but this we know, when Christ appears we shall become like him.' 'God shared our manhood that we might share his Godhead' – for time and eternity. Amen.